# BEYONCÉGRAPHICA

First published in 2017 by Aurum Press,
an imprint of The Quarto Group.
The Old Brewery, 6 Blundell Street,
London N7 9BH, United Kingdom.
www.QuartoKnows.com

© 2017 Quarto Publishing plc.
Text by Chris Roberts
Design by Gemma Wilson
Illustrations by Marco Giannini (pages 8–9, 19, 63, 66–67, 72, 74–75, 86–87, 92–93, 95, 98–99, 106–107, 122–123, 126–127, 134–135, 152–153, 154–155, 158–159, 164–165, 170–171, 178–179, 184, 191, 192–193, 200–201, 212–213, 216–217, 226–227, 240, 243, 246).

A catalogue record for this book is available from the British Library.

ISBN 978 1 78131 651 1

10 9 8 7 6 5 4 3 2 1
2021 2020 2019 2018 2017

Printed in China

## DATA SOURCES

Where applicable, data is correct up to the end of 2016.
Data from IMDB 8–9, 12–13,
Data from Verywell.com 14
Data from Fusion.net 19, 170–171
Data from Billboard 28–29
Data from Glamourmagazine.co.uk 37
Data from Wikipedia 42–43, 46, 66–67, 86–87, 92–93, 98–99, 106–107, 122–123, 154–155, 158–159, 200–201, 216–217, 232, 240, 243
Data from www.theRinger.com 50, 184
Data from www.Setlist.fm 63, 72, 134–135
Data from www.YouTube.com 74–75, 95, 164–165, 192–193
Data from www.Forbes.com 103, 144–145
Data from www.LATimes.com 103
Data from www.Louievreveals.com 115
Data from www.Looktothestars.org 126–127
Data from www.Radiox.co.uk 152
Data from www.VH1.com 152
Data from www.NME.com 152
Data from www.Complex.com 152
Data from www.Flavorwire.com 152
Data from www.concerthotels.com 170–171, 226
Data from www.grammy.com 178–179,
Data from www.thebeyhive.tumblr.com 184
Data from www.thequeenbey.tumblr.com 184
Data from www.thebeyhive.tumblr.com 184
Data from www.facebook.com/beyonce 184
Data from www.people.com 191
Data from www.celebuzz.com 212–213
Data from www.DailyMirror.com 212–213
Data from www.ibtimes.co.uk 228
Data from http://madamenoire.com 228
Data from www.belfasttelegraph.co.uk 228
Data from http://zumic.com 240
Data from www.dailymail.co.uk 243
Data from http://fashionista.com 243
Data from http://www.bustle.com 245
Data from http://www.breakingnews.ie 246
Data from http://www.statista.com 246

# BEYONCÉGRAPHICA

## A GRAPHIC BIOGRAPHY OF BEYONCÉ

Chris Roberts

# CONTENTS

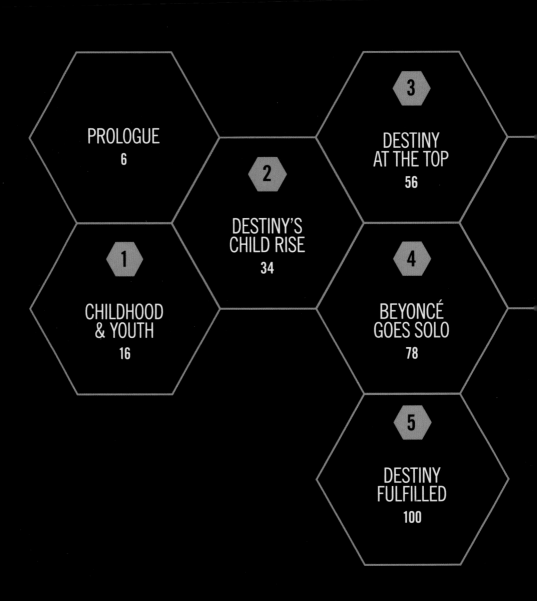

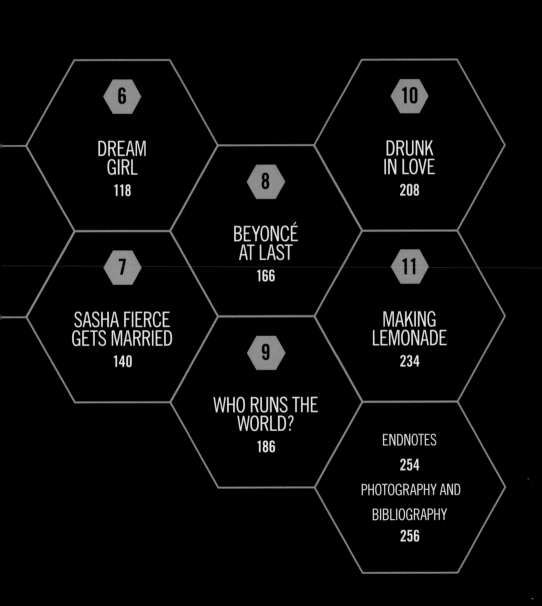

# PROLOGUE

'I'm over being a pop star. I don't want to be a hot girl. I want to be iconic. I feel like I've accomplished a lot. I feel like I'm highly respected, which is more important than any award or any amount of records. And I feel like there's a point when being a pop star is not enough.'

As Beyoncé's career approaches the two-decade mark at the highest level, there can be no doubt that she's popular entertainment's biggest icon of the twenty-first century. More than a mere pop star. She's sold over one hundred million records as a solo artist and, prior to that, another sixty million with Destiny's Child (one of the biggest-selling girl groups of all time). She's been nominated for more Grammy Awards than any woman in history, and won twenty-two. She was the top-selling artist and the most-played on radio of the 2000s, and has been listed by *Forbes* as the most powerful woman in entertainment. Her marriage to Jay-Z has established her as half of one of the most influential couples in America, even counting the Obamas as pals, with Beyoncé chosen to sing at the presidential inauguration. More recently she's added political activism, philanthropy and feminism to her range, notably supporting the Black Lives Matter campaign. She's inspired countless articles and theses about who she is, what she represents, what she means.

**'WHEN YOU'RE FAMOUS, NO ONE LOOKS AT YOU AS HUMAN ANY MORE. YOU BECOME THE PROPERTY OF THE PUBLIC.'**

'When you're famous,' she said in late 2014, 'no one looks at you as human any more. You become the property of the public. There's nothing real about it. You can't put your finger on who I am. I can't put my finger on who I am. I am complicated. I've been through a lot.'

At the same time, she's promoted her image through everything from Pepsi to Hilfiger, Topshop to L'Oréal, cleverly retaining her air of above-it-all class.

**LEFT:** Queen Bey strutting her stuff in Sacramento, performing songs from her album *I Am… Sasha Fierce* in 2009.

# REACH FOR
## *the stars*

We know that Queen Bey is at the top of her league when it comes to musical success, but how does she measure up against her fellow female artists when it comes to height? She reportedly stands at 5 foot 6.5 inches, so she's sitting pretty in the middle.

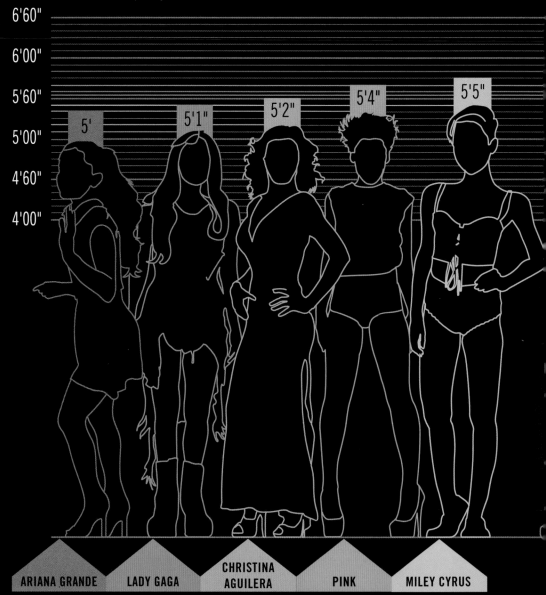

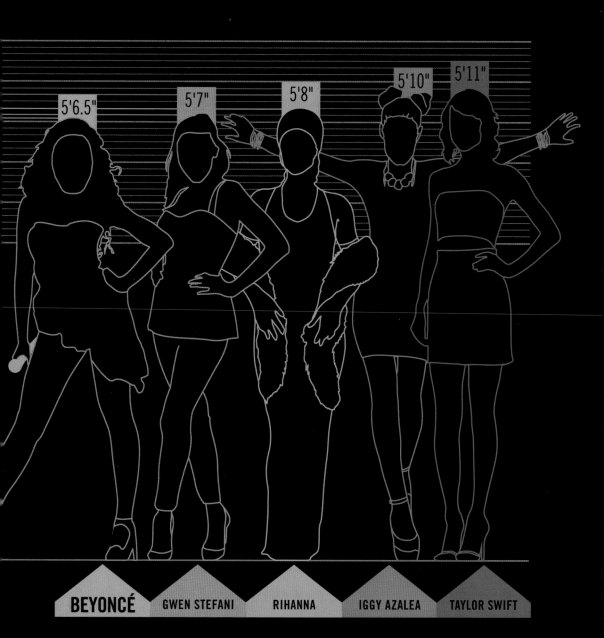

5'6.5"  5'7"  5'8"  5'10"  5'11"

**BEYONCÉ**  GWEN STEFANI  RIHANNA  IGGY AZALEA  TAYLOR SWIFT

While her film career may have been varied, from the triumph of *Dreamgirls* to *Obsessed* (touching on most points between), her musical output has matured and evolved significantly. It has graduated from the blistering solo breakthrough of 'Crazy in Love', via the identity shifts of *I Am… Sasha Fierce*, to the darker, more challenging themes and rhythms of 2013's *Beyoncé* and 2016's candid, critic-conquering *Lemonade*. The *New Yorker* hailed 'Her Highness' as 'the most important and compelling popular musician of the twenty-first century – the result, the logical end point … of pop'.

Iconic? Beyoncé is as big as they get, and just keeps on getting bigger. 'I don't like to gamble,' she's said, 'but if there's one thing I'm willing to bet on, it's myself.'

The halo seems secure and the formation is solid. We can safely double down on Beyoncé's stellar status and pop pre-eminence. She's come a long, long way since her birth in Houston, Texas, as the Eighties kicked into gear, in September 1981.

Her dad, Mathew, a Xerox salesman, would famously go on to manage his daughter. Her mother, Celestine, owned a hairdressing salon. And her younger sister, Solange, has made her own headway. Unsurprisingly, Beyoncé Giselle Knowles was a hit in dancing and singing classes at school, winning her first talent contest at age seven later attending a performing arts high school.

## 'I DON'T LIKE TO GAMBLE, BUT IF THERE'S ONE THING I'M WILLING TO BET ON, IT'S MYSELF.'

She and young friend Kelly Rowland joined their first girl group, Girls Tyme, as kids, before Mathew decided to get serious and almost literally bet the house on his daughter becoming a star. 'We were waking up every morning, singing all day and loving every minute of it,' Beyoncé has said. A record deal finally gave the girls the platform they needed, and Beyoncé turned that platform into a global stage.

Destiny's Child – as they became known in 1994 – first nibbled at the charts in 1997 with 'No, No, No Part 1' before receiving public affirmation with the likes of 'Say My Name', 'Bills, Bills, Bills' and 'Jumpin', Jumpin''. Line-up changes ensued and the trio of Knowles, Rowland and Michelle Williams hit the next level with international smashes and indelible pop hits such as 'Independent Women', 'Survivor' (also the name of their third album) and 'Bootylicious'.

Much like Diana Ross parting ways with The Supremes in an earlier era, Beyoncé was encouraged to go solo. At first not every step was an unqualified success – though her role as Foxxy Cleopatra in the Austin Powers franchise certainly raised her profile – then, after a telling (in retrospect) feature spot on Jay-Z's '03 Bonnie & Clyde', the 2003 album *Dangerously in Love* pushed the green light on her superstar status. 'Crazy in Love' led the charge, pursued by 'Baby Boy' and 'Naughty Girl'. Five Grammys and a tour alongside Missy Elliott and Alicia Keys sealed the appeal, and Houston had only one hometown heroine in mind to sing the national anthem at the Super Bowl in February 2004.

The Destiny's Child name was revisited for one more album, *Destiny Fulfilled*, before it became clear that Beyoncé's star was too hot to contain within a collective. Her second solo album, *B'Day*, coincided with her twenty-fifth birthday, and sold like, well, hot birthday cakes. Lead single 'Déjà Vu' featured that man Jay-Z. Further film roles followed, with the musical *Dreamgirls* – loosely based on The Supremes' story – succeeding both commercially and critically.

She just kept ascending. Her marriage to Jay-Z in 2008 preceded the paradigm shift of the *I Am... Sasha Fierce* album, which introduced the concept of Beyoncé's extroverted alter ego, who she nurtured to overcome stage fright. As Beyoncé herself has admitted, 'I'm not like her in real life at all.' It also gave us 'Single Ladies (Put a Ring on It)', an iconic song with, arguably, an even more iconic video. (It was this video that led to an unforgettable, slightly excruciating episode at an awards ceremony, involving Kanye West and Taylor Swift.) A duet with Lady Gaga ('Telephone') provided another zeitgeist-capturing flourish before Beyoncé took a nine-month break to travel and 'be inspired by things again'.

When she returned her mystique had only grown and she was the one doing the inspiring. In 2011 she became the first female solo artist to headline the Glastonbury Festival in over twenty years. Her album *4* yielded the impactful 'Run the World (Girls)', and 2012 began with another Carter girl introduced to the world as Beyoncé gave birth to her first child, Blue Ivy Carter. The next world tour, which ran to 132 dates, bore the keenly debated name The Mrs. Carter Show World Tour.

Her exalted status was now such that she could ignore certain tried and trusted career path 'rules', and rewrite the textbooks. Her fifth album, *Beyoncé*,

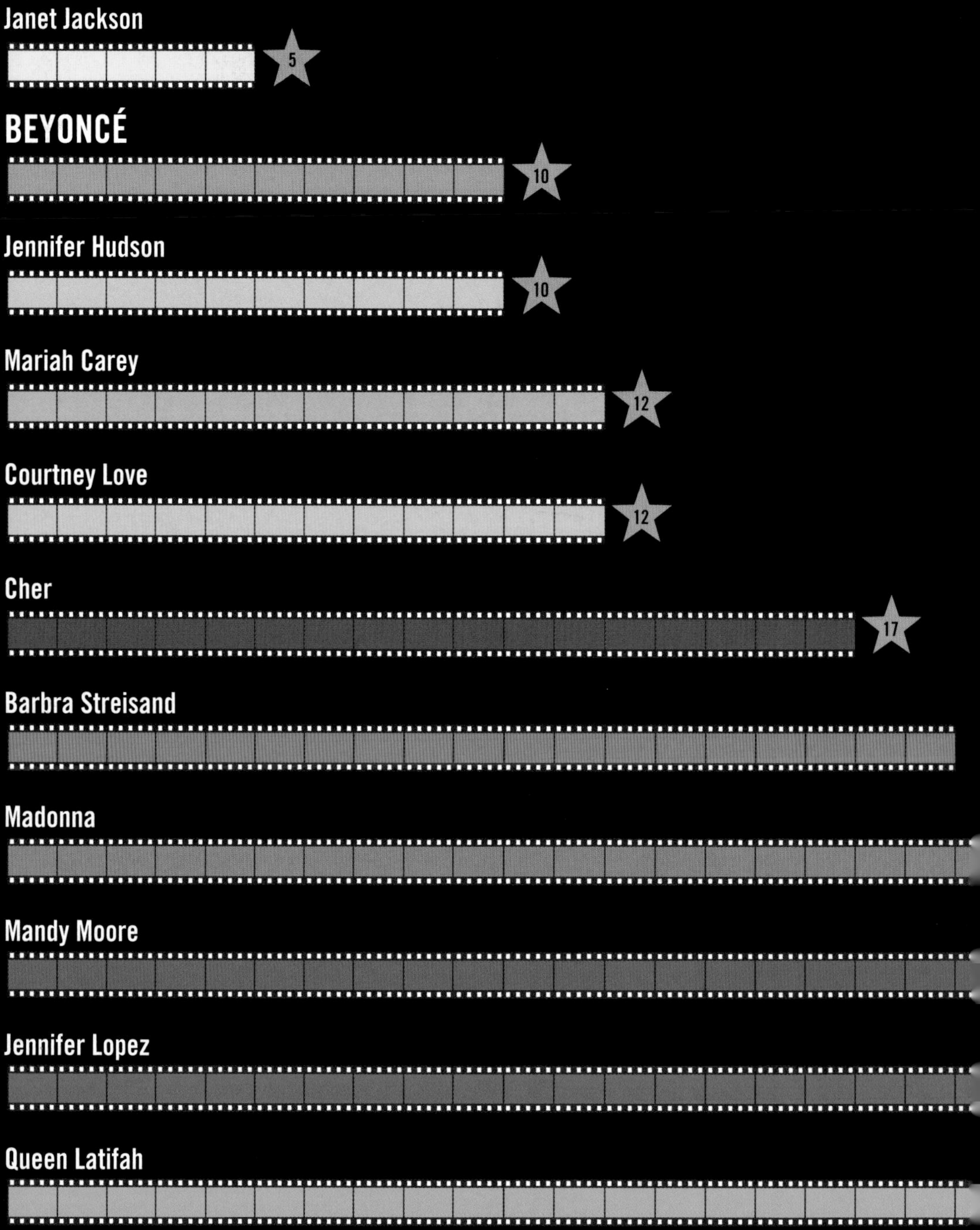

**Janet Jackson**

5

# BEYONCÉ

10

**Jennifer Hudson**

10

**Mariah Carey**

12

**Courtney Love**

12

**Cher**

17

**Barbra Streisand**

**Madonna**

**Mandy Moore**

**Jennifer Lopez**

**Queen Latifah**

was released without any advance fanfare and stunned fans with its subversive distinctly non-mainstream electro-R&B rhythms and intimate, confessional lyrics. 'Drunk in love', she and Jay-Z toured stadiums together. In 2016 she broke the mould with an even bolder statement, debuting new song 'Formation' at the Super Bowl half-time show. Subsequent album *Lemonade* doubled as a movie and made Beyoncé the first artist to have her first six albums top the Billboard charts in their opening week. It also garnered some of the most glowing reviews in popular music's history. 'The queen … makes her most powerful, ambitious statement yet,' wrote *Rolling Stone*.

Of course with the Beyoncé phenomenon, it's about more than 'just' the music. In terms of cultural resonance, and taking in buzz-worthy bullet points from fashion to feminism, from businesswoman to black empowerment, Beyoncé is probably the biggest, most talked- and written-about icon of our times. Her strength is much proclaimed and admired. In reality, she has overcome the heartbreaks of a miscarriage and depression that many women who aren't under such scrutiny of the spotlight struggle to deal with.

## ALL THE WORLD IS *a stage*

Beyoncé is not the only female singer who has been attracted by the bright lights of Hollywood. Some of these divas started their careers as actresses and made the move to singing, like Jennifer Lopez, but however they made it to the silver screen, it's clear that among them they've starred in an impressive number of movies

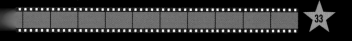

She and Jay-Z are a couple under constant and intense public examination who nonetheless manage to misdirect with cunning smokescreens. 'I'm learning how to drown out the constant noise that is such an inseparable part of my life,' this muse to so many has said. 'I don't have to prove anything to anyone. I only have to follow my heart and concentrate on what I want to say to the world. I run my world.'

## TWINNING *is winning*

Beyoncé took her fans by surprise and the world's media by storm when she announced in February 2017 that she was expecting twins. And she's in good company: these celebrity couples are just some of the showbiz stars who have been twice blessed.

BEYONCÉ + JAY-Z

MARIAH CAREY + NICK CANNON

*Monroe & Moroccan Scott*

CELINE DION + RENÉ ANGELIL

*Eddy & Nelson*

JENNIFER LOPEZ + MARC ANTHONY

*Max & Emme*

SARAH JESSICA PARKER + MATTHEW BRODERICK

*Marion Loretta Elwell & Tabitha Hodge*

ANGELINA JOLIE + BRAD PITT

*Knox Leon & Vivienne Marcheline*

JULIA ROBERTS + DANNY MODER

*Hazel & Phinnaeus*

She broke the internet yet again on 1 February 2017, announcing her pregnancy with twins in spectacular style. She revealed her baby bump in a much-discussed Instagram post, which featured her pictured in front of a wall of roses, dressed in mismatched underwear and a tulle veil. Everything about it was analysed, from her 'subversion of the male gaze' to whether clashing lingerie was the new fashion must-have. And this just twelve days before she was to perform at the Grammys, where she was nominated for nine awards.

There, too, motherhood was a central theme: she was introduced in a striking tableau featuring her own mother, Tina Knowles, and her daughter, Blue Ivy, all three women regally attired in robes of gold. And although she went home with two awards – for Best Urban Contemporary Album for *Lemonade* and Best Music Video for 'Formation' – there could be no doubting that it was her night. When Adele took the top gong for Record of the Year, the British star insisted the award be dedicated to Beyoncé, going so far as to split it

## 'I KNOW THAT, YES, I AM POWERFUL.'

in half to share it with her idol, whose album *Lemonade* she described as 'so monumental and so well thought-out and so beautiful and soul-bearing.' As Beyonce wiped away a tear, Adele told her 'You are our light… I love you. I always have. And I always will.'

Adele's not the only one. The arrival of two new members of the Carter-Knowles clan is unlikely to do anything to dull our appetite for all things Queen Bey, be they music or fashion. When a new Ivy Park collection for Top Shop was announced in February, the *Guardian*'s fashion correspondent swooned, 'Beyoncé is the spiritual leader of 21st century womankind… When she makes an announcement, the world listens.'

Queen Bey continues to slay. Perhaps she runs the pop-cultural world; we just live in it. Within this book we'll tell her life story, documenting her rise to fame and even giddier rise thereafter.

'I know that, yes, I am powerful,' she has said, apparently astonished rather than arrogant about everything she's achieved. 'I'm more powerful than my mind can even digest and understand.' Let's try to digest and understand how she came to embrace that power.

# CHILDHOOD & YOUTH

Queen Bey was born on 4 September 1981, in Houston, Texas. The date would have special significance for her, as she revealed thirty years later: 'We all have special numbers in our lives, and four is that for me. It's the day I was born. My mother's birthday and a lot of my friends' birthdays are on the fourth. April fourth is my wedding date.' But, in 1981, all of that lay in the future, and few people could have predicted the glittering horizon that awaited when the Knowles' first child, Beyoncé Giselle, made her grand entrance at Houston's Park Plaza Hospital.

Her parents, perhaps, had an early inkling. Beyoncé has suggested that she was born with music coursing through her veins. 'My dad tells me that as a baby I would go crazy whenever I heard music, and I tried to dance before I could walk. He has the embarrassing videos to prove it!' she confessed in an autobiography of Destiny's Child, *Soul Survivors*, written twenty years later.

As for her mother, she 'claims it was an easy and relatively painless birth, unlike some of my other entrances,' laughed Beyoncé. Easy it may have been, but it still earned her mother the right to name the baby – the new parents had agreed, Beyoncé said, that 'Dad would pick my middle name and my mom would choose my first name. So Beyoncé comes from her – it's actually her maiden name.' Or a version of it, at least. Celestine 'Tina' Ann Beyincé was keen for her French family name to survive, though her own father, Beyoncé's grandpa, Lumiz Beyincé, was less convinced by the unconventional choice. He argued that the child would be 'really mad' because 'that's a last name'. And, indeed, Beyoncé did dislike her name in her early years. With time, she grew to love it, but, she has explained, 'when I was little, it was just another excuse for kids to pick on me. Every morning when the teacher took roll call, I wanted to crawl under my desk.' At home she answered to the nickname 'Bey', or just 'B'.

# SAY MY *name*

Beyoncé's unusual name was invented by her parents and is based on her mother's maiden name, Beyincé. These baby bottles represent the number of babies who have been named after Beyoncé in the US and the years in which the popularity of the name peaked.

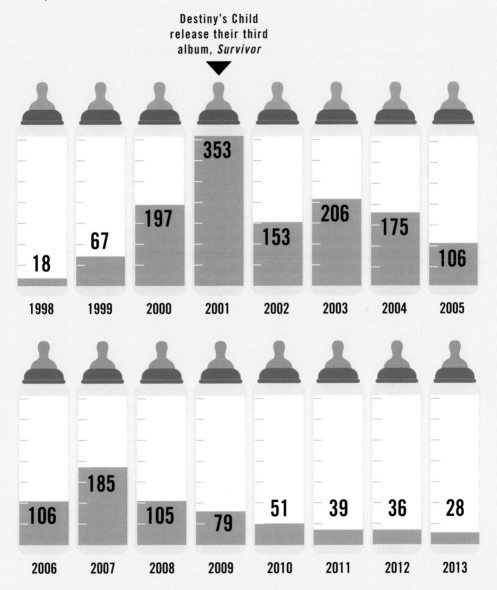

Destiny's Child release their third album, *Survivor*

| | | | | | | | |
|---|---|---|---|---|---|---|---|
| 18 | 67 | 197 | 353 | 153 | 206 | 175 | 106 |
| 1998 | 1999 | 2000 | 2001 | 2002 | 2003 | 2004 | 2005 |
| 106 | 185 | 105 | 79 | 51 | 39 | 36 | 28 |
| 2006 | 2007 | 2008 | 2009 | 2010 | 2011 | 2012 | 2013 |

Her parents, Mathew and Tina, both loved singing and had themselves taken part in talent shows in their youth. Tina had even sung in a Supremes-inspired pop group, The Beltones, designing the costumes herself. The couple's influence on Beyoncé and their involvement in her subsequent career path cannot be overstated, and it began early on.

Mathew was born in 1952 in Gadsden, Alabama. His father ran a scrap metal business and drove trucks, while his mother was a quilt-maker and a maid for a white family. Racism was rife in the southern states, but Mathew became one of the first African-American children to go to Litchfield Junior High School in Marion. As an indication of the tensions of the times, around the passing of the Civil Rights Act in 1964 he had to have state troopers escort him to school. A basketball scholarship got him to the University of Tennessee in Chattanooga. Almost inevitably, as a black teenager in the Sixties, he engaged with politics and joined demonstrations. Importantly, he also realized that studying and working hard were key to breaking society's less welcome patterns.

He transferred to Fisk University in Nashville, a leading black university, as the Seventies dawned. Interest piqued by Berry Gordy's breakthroughs with the Motown label, he honed his knowledge of the business side of music, graduating with degrees in economics and management. He moved through various professional sales roles – at one point selling life insurance, at another medical supplies – until he settled with a job for the Xerox company. Xerox was then a Rochester, New York-based corporation, which had given the world the first plain-paper photocopier, and was now introducing the laser printer. Mathew did well, and by the late Eighties was earning a six-figure salary.

Tina was two years his junior. Born in Galveston, Texas (a town made famous by Glen Campbell's version of the titular Jimmy Webb song) in January 1954, her heritage included, on her mother Agnéz's side, Jewish American, Choctaw, African-American and Louisiana Creole, and, on her father Lumiz's side, Chinese, Indonesian, Spanish and French. More simply, Tina in later years tended to describe them to interviewers as just 'Louisiana Creole'. Her mother was the youngest of fifteen.

At junior high Tina sang in The Beltones and designed costumes, which her mother, a talented seamstress, would then create. Agnéz taught Tina much about economical dressmaking, skills that Tina would put to good use in later years with Destiny's Child and which she recognized as 'a blessing'. Upon leaving school, Tina worked in a bank. Like Mathew, she was motivated by music and a desire for social justice, citing Marvin Gaye's *What's Going On* as one of her favourite records. 'It's a masterpiece,' she said. 'For the first time, young people started becoming more aware of things that were going on in the world and how they could make a difference, rather than just being concerned with looking good and partying. It was such a conscious record. I spent so many hours as a seventeen-year-old listening to it.'

The Knowles and the Beyoncé families relocated to Houston, America's fourth largest city, in the late Seventies. It was a place famed for oil and NASA's mission control – and not, perhaps, the most obvious hometown for a future superstar. Mathew and Tina met at a party, where the chemistry was immediately apparent. When they then bumped into each other the next day, a dinner invitation ensued. They married in 1980, when Mathew was twenty-eight and Tina twenty-six. The arrival of Beyoncé a little under two years later gave them cause to celebrate, and further motivation to do well by their burgeoning family. Tina opened an upmarket hair salon, Headliners, which proved a huge success, and soon the family had moved to a six-bedroom house in an affluent, racially mixed area of town. Sister Solange Piaget Knowles was born in 1986.

> **'THEY'RE JUST SISTERS LIKE ANY OTHER SISTERS – AND THEY LOVE AND SUPPORT EACH OTHER.'**
> **TINA KNOWLES**

The five years between the two girls meant that Beyoncé helped Tina out with looking after the infant Solange. Their mother claims they very rarely argued. 'There was a period,' she's admitted to *Access Hollywood*, 'where Solange got on Beyoncé's nerves because she was in all her stuff, just the typical things kids go through, but they have always been very protective of each other and very close. There's never been this rivalry stuff that people sometimes try to make out. They're just sisters like any other sisters – and they love and support each other.'

Music filled their home on leafy Parkwood Drive. (Beyoncé retained affection for her childhood home to the extent that she later named her management team Parkwood.) The parents sang to their children and from infancy Beyoncé went 'crazy' whenever she heard music. Mathew and Tina's favourites included

# MEAT LOAF

JESSICA & ASHLEE SIMPSON

B.B. KING

CLINT BLACK

# USHER

# THE JONAS ☆ BROTHERS

## ERYKAH BADU

## SELENA GOMEZ

## KELLY CLARKSON

MIRANDA LAMBERT

BUDDY HOLLY

JANIS JOPLIN

STEVIE RAY VAUGHAN

## CIARA

VANILLA ICE

## TEXAS *y'all*

Although her hometown of Houston, Texas, can't take any credit for Beyoncé's success, there's no doubt that the Lone Star State produces some excellent musical talent.

the soul sounds of the Philadelphia label, Barry White, Motown and of course Marvin Gaye as well as the jazz giants Duke Ellington and Count Basie. The new decade saw Michael Jackson, Prince and Luther Vandross taking turns on the turntable.

At St Mary's Elementary School, Beyoncé immediately gravitated towards dance, whether it was ballet or jazz. One afternoon she rushed home from first grade to sing her mother a new song she'd just learned, standing at the kitchen table to deliver her performance. Already she was a natural entertainer. 'I'll never forget that feeling,' she recalled later. 'I loved performing for my mom – it was a rush.'

The sisters have spoken of colourful Christmases with all the frills and eating 'fried Snickers bars' as a once-a-year treat. Solange has stated that they weren't allowed overly expensive clothes and that, despite how well their parents had done, their mother retained a keen eye for flea market bargains. For extra pocket money, little Beyoncé would sweep the floor at the salon. She seems to have developed a strong work ethic at a young age – though it was combined with a sense of fun and adventure that would also go on to inform her later career. She loved the rides and rollercoasters at the Houston theme park Six Flags AstroWorld. Every Sunday meant a family visit to their local Methodist church, and Beyoncé sang gospel in the choir from the age of seven.

Already the sisters excelled as performers. They'd even sell tickets for home shows, making impromptu stages out of the furniture. These shows were 'a big part of their lives,' Tina has laughed, and Beyoncé, from a young age, took them seriously. Solange recalls her big sister practising in front of the bedroom mirror. 'I specifically remember her taking a line out of a song or a routine and just doing it over and over and over again until it was perfect.'

Aged five, in 1986, Beyoncé attended her first concert, and, it being a Michael Jackson show, it was no forgettable night. 'That night I decided exactly my purpose,' she told a TV interviewer years on. 'He's the reason I do what I do. I'd never have experienced that magic if it wasn't for him.' Home video footage has shown Beyoncé around this time self-assuredly rapping to camera:

'I think I'm bad / Beyoncé's my name / Love is my game.' On the other hand, she was shy at school. Teasing about her name didn't help, and as she said to MTV later, 'I was the type of child who, if someone didn't like me, it killed me.' The jibes stung. One boy who sat next to her called her 'dumb and stupid and ugly', she remembered. She took to dressing blandly, trying to avoid attention, though some misinterpreted her reticence. 'People thought I was stuck-up. Some people misunderstand quietness and shyness and think you're full of yourself.' We can perhaps already discern the roots of – and the personal necessity for – the Sasha Fierce persona here.

However, by the time she reached the age of seven, Beyoncé was excelling in dance lessons. Mathew and Tina had hired an extra tutor to boost her academic studies, but it was in the school dance classes that her stellar potential was first noted. Her teacher at the time, Darlette Johnson, said, 'I knew she was a star, I knew it. She hit a note and I said, "Sing that again!" Her parents came to pick her up and I said, "She can really sing!"' Other than Mathew and Tina, Johnson would become one of Beyoncé's earliest and most ardent champions. Beyoncé has acknowledged the debt she owes her early teacher: 'She told me to perform at a talent show and I fell in love with the stage. I owe a lot to her.' It wasn't just Johnson's faith in Beyoncé that made a difference, it was also her talent as a teacher. 'Miss Darlette … could get anybody to dance,' Beyoncé said. 'Aside from basic moves, she taught me self-esteem, confidence, a positive attitude and, most importantly, discipline.'

## 'I'LL NEVER FORGET THAT FEELING… I LOVED PERFORMING FOR MY MOM – IT WAS A RUSH.'

Still, after entering the school talent show at Johnson's encouragement, Beyoncé was at first extremely nervous. 'I was terrified and I didn't wanna do it, and she [Johnson] was like: "Come on, baby, get out there!" I walked out and I was scared, but when the music started I don't know what happened … I just … changed.' Fierce!

Mathew's pep talk had possibly helped too. Beyoncé sang John Lennon's 'Imagine', having been coached by her father in what the lyrics meant. He'd even shown the little girl a picture of Martin Luther King. She not only won the contest (against older teenagers) but earned a standing ovation.

**ABOVE LEFT:** Beyoncé and her father, Mathew Knowles, at the premiere of *Austin Powers in Goldmember* in 2002.

**ABOVE RIGHT:** Beyoncé and her mother, Tina Knowles, at *MTV's Total Request Live*, November 2005.

Her parents were caught between amazement and glee. 'She was a sweet but shy kid,' Tina recalled, 'but when she got onstage and sang "Imagine" we couldn't believe it was the same kid! Her confidence came out.' Mathew has put it even more emphatically, telling *Billboard*, 'Her mother and I looked at each other and said: "That can't be our Beyoncé; she's so shy and quiet" … but she was a different person onstage.' It was a revelation for everyone, including Beyoncé herself. From that moment on, she realized 'that's how I expressed myself – through music. I only felt comfortable when I was singing or dancing.' Her parents recognized that their daughter had found something that let her be herself and were wise enough to let her pursue it. 'She came alive,' Tina said simply. 'That's kind of how it all started. We encouraged her to do this, because it brought out her personality.'

Unsurprisingly they entered their daughter into a stream of subsequent talent contests. Mathew reckons she took part in around thirty, and won them all. She was even nominated for a prestigious Houston arts award. In 1990 she went to the Cynthia Ann Parker Elementary School, a Houston school with an emphasis on music, where Beyoncé received vocal coaching as part of her lessons. From there she moved to the High School for the Performing and Visual Arts and then the Elsik High School. Her parents even arranged vocal coaching with an international opera tenor, David Lee Brewer. 'What she let loose was one of the most impressive sounds I'd ever heard from a child,' he said later. 'Something about it grabbed me and wouldn't let me go. The sound was molten gold, with a distinguished timbre. This was more than just a voice, I thought, it was a spirit.' Brewer was invited to move into an apartment above the Knowles' garage, so seriously were the family now taking their girl's gift. Though it wasn't all hard work: they also bought her a karaoke machine to sing along to her R&B favourites. 'Karaoke was my joy!' she confided to an interviewer. 'I'd be with it all day and tape myself singing over other people's songs.'

While she was competent rather than outstanding academically, she now knew her point of focus, and her parents were backing her all the way. Her alter ego also had her back, as it was around this time that she adopted the feisty Sasha Fierce persona – a name initially given to her by her cousin Angie – to get her through bouts of stage fright and the pressure she felt now that everybody expected her to be effortlessly fantastic at such a young age. Sasha was 'confident and fearless and can do a lot of things that I can't do. She protects me,' said Beyoncé.

Beyoncé was ready to deploy that fearless, protective instinct for those close to her, too, engaging her fierce alter ego if ever anyone at school tried to intimidate her kid sister. Solange remembers that Beyoncé 'threatened to put some hands on [other kids] if they bothered me in junior high'. The protective instinct clearly runs deep through their relationship – and would remain in evidence when both were adults, with Solange ready to get Beyoncé's back the way her big sister always got hers. 'I always felt the need to love and protect her,' Beyoncé told *Harper's Bazaar* of her little sister. 'Our differences added to our friendship. The love I have for her is indescribable. Disrespect my sister, and I will go completely crazy on you!'

By now the sisters had plenty of friends outside the family. But Beyoncé was to meet some new ones, as the first seeds of what was eventually to blossom as Destiny's Child were sown. LaTavia Roberson was a classmate at Parker Elementary School and also a much-praised dancer. By 1990, Beyoncé had won a plethora of trophies already, and she bonded with Roberson, who was two months younger, at a visual and performing arts workshop affiliated with Texas Southern University. The pair hit it off, and formed off-the-cuff groups with other pals, performing in front of school friends. When a local entrepreneur, Andretta Tillman, invited Beyoncé and LaTavia to audition for a kids' girl group she'd envisaged, Mathew and Tina worked on prepping them for their audition.

Out of sixty or seventy wannabes, the two friends were chosen to be teamed up with three other pre-teen girls. They were given the moniker Girls Tyme, Houston's youthful all-singing, all-dancing would-be answer to En Vogue. Joining them in the confirmed line-up were the sisters Nikki and Nina Taylor – LaTavia's cousins – and Ashley Támar Davis. In the coming years, the members chopped and changed quite a bit, but Beyoncé was a fixture as lead vocalist, with Andretta Tillman funding and managing the group. And then LaTavia brought a new girl into the equation – one Kelly Rowland.

Urged on by Tillman, the girls rehearsed frequently, often half-trashing bedrooms and the family living room with their enthusiastic dance moves and high kicks. Tina's hair salon was another practice venue. 'We made them cut

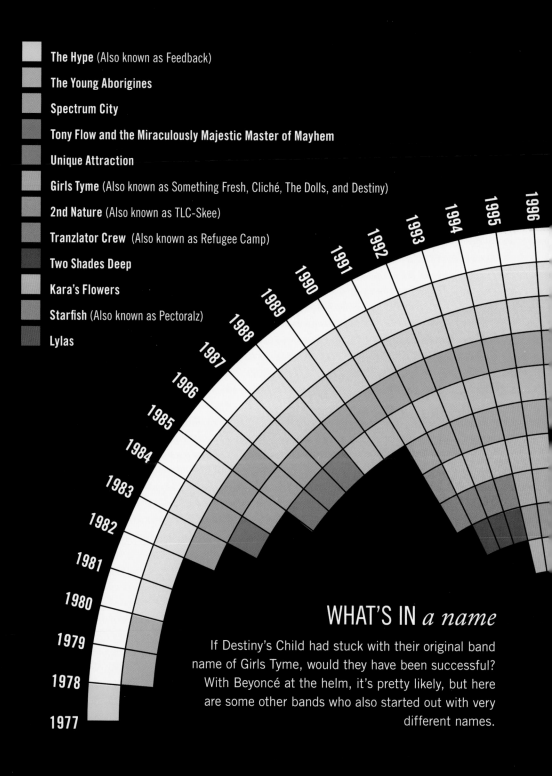

The Hype (Also known as Feedback)

The Young Aborigines

Spectrum City

Tony Flow and the Miraculously Majestic Master of Mayhem

Unique Attraction

Girls Tyme (Also known as Something Fresh, Cliché, The Dolls, and Destiny)

2nd Nature (Also known as TLC-Skee)

Tranzlator Crew (Also known as Refugee Camp)

Two Shades Deep

Kara's Flowers

Starfish (Also known as Pectoralz)

Lylas

1977 1978 1979 1980 1981 1982 1983 1984 1985 1986 1987 1988 1989 1990 1991 1992 1993 1994 1995 1996

# WHAT'S IN *a name*

If Destiny's Child had stuck with their original band name of Girls Tyme, would they have been successful? With Beyoncé at the helm, it's pretty likely, but here are some other bands who also started out with very different names.

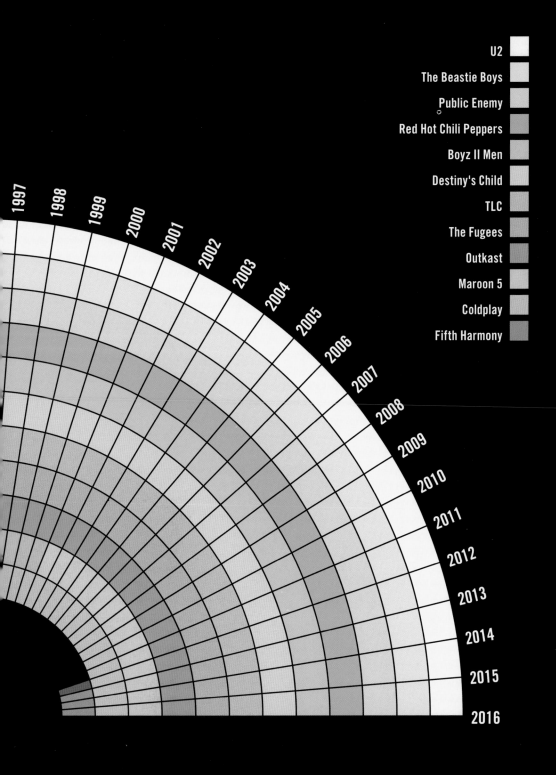

1997
1998
1999
2000
2001
2002
2003
2004
2005
2006
2007
2008
2009
2010
2011
2012
2013
2014
2015
2016

U2
The Beastie Boys
Public Enemy
Red Hot Chili Peppers
Boyz II Men
Destiny's Child
TLC
The Fugees
Outkast
Maroon 5
Coldplay
Fifth Harmony

**ABOVE:** Mathew Knowles, Kelly Rowland and Tina Knowles at the 45th Annual Grammy Awards.

off the hair dryers,' Beyoncé chuckled. 'It was like: "We're about to perform! Everything has to shut off!"' Tina has recalled that the girls would shout out 'Put your hands together!' and the customers 'would be rolling their eyes. That was a tough audience.' Mathew, meanwhile, would solicit opinions as to what aspects of their act needed to be improved. Beyoncé needed no persuading in the pursuit of perfection. Janet Jackson had always been a major role model, but when Beyoncé heard the then-new star Mariah Carey sing, she was instantly set on mimicking her melismatic vocal techniques.

For Kelly Rowland it was Whitney Houston who was the great pop idol, and, despite Kelly's contrasting early life, her part in the story of Destiny's Child and Beyoncé's own evolution cannot be overstated. She was born Kelendria, seven months before Beyoncé, and, when the two young girls first met, Kelly and her mother had just moved from Atlanta to Houston. She'd displayed vocal chops since impressing in the church choir as a four-year-old. However, her upbringing hadn't been quite as blessed as Beyoncé's. Doris, her mother, had to leave her hard-drinking, ill-tempered father, and struggled for money as a nanny. Once they were in Houston, Kelly hardly ever saw her father. 'I would look at kids at school being picked up by their dads and that was something I missed,' she told the *Daily Mail* decades later. 'Music was my escape. It still is.'

The Knowles family embraced Kelly and before long she'd stay over a few nights a week. It's been occasionally reported that they 'adopted' her, but that wasn't the case. She and Beyoncé just loved singing together, and bonded fiercely. Kelly has said that when they shared a room it was a noisy slumber party every time. They and the other girls in the group would study old videos by the Jackson Five and The Supremes, while Tina worked on styling them and designing costumes. They were taking this seriously, planning the ultimate pop package.

However, this wasn't some kind of pushy-parent boot camp. According to Beyoncé, it was always primarily about fun. The rehearsals, dance routines, vocal arrangements? 'It seemed like playtime,' she said.

Playtime extended when Kelly moved in full-time in 1991, and started calling Mathew and Tina 'Uncle' and 'Auntie'. Beyoncé and Kelly have come to refer to each other as cousins. 'I'm so blessed to have had the Knowleses in my life when I was growing up,' Kelly has said, crediting them with not only providing a family environment, but also structure. 'Tina would just look at me and say,

"Girl, you shouldn't have an attitude like that,'" Kelly remembered. Beyoncé could vouch for this. 'There's nobody can keep you in check like my mom and dad,' she said. 'Especially my mom. I have the type of mom that, even if you're not her child, she tells you the truth.'

It suited all parties, including Kelly's mother. While some tabloids have since tried to make an issue of it, Kelly has stated that her mother's schedule as a live-in nanny didn't permit her to transport her daughter to rehearsals and back every day. Initially all agreed that Kelly could stay with the Knowleses for the summer, but the arrangement just sat comfortably for longer. Kelly's mother, Doris, had a key to the house and would visit every night, often staying over at weekends, and Kelly has described the set-up as 'a big, old happy family ... I say I have three parents, Tina and Mathew and my mom. Three wise people to help me.' And, alongside the wisdom she found in the Knowles' household, Kelly has also admitted that 'there was always financial security at Beyoncé's house'. With Tina's hair salon doing a roaring trade, Kelly said, 'I was so grateful that I didn't have to move all around any more.' By 2002, Kelly confessed that she called Mathew 'Dad'.

> ### 'I'M SO BLESSED TO HAVE HAD THE KNOWLESES IN MY LIFE WHEN I WAS GROWING UP.'
> **KELLY ROWLAND**

Beyoncé and Kelly geed each other up, 'singing all day and loving every minute of it', listening to the likes of SWV (Sisters With Voices), Jodeci and Guy. By this time, it was clear that Beyoncé was more than just another wannabe. On a home video she recorded a list of her goals. In startling detail, rather than just expressing the common wish to be famous, she detailed her ambition to make a gold record, then a platinum follow-up, and then to write and produce her third. Remarkably, she'd ticked all these off her list before the age of twenty-one.

But all that was still to come. At the mere age of ten and eleven years, there were such things as set backs. Andretta Tillman entered Girls Tyme for the long-running TV show *Star Search*. 'We were kind of nervous,' recalled LaTavia later. 'They made us do a rap song, even though we wanted to sing. They even invented a new hip-hop category for us.' Famously, the girls didn't win. 'It hurt so bad to lose,' Kelly remembered. 'But we were still smiling. Then, when we walked offstage, everybody just broke down and was crying. Imagine – ten- and eleven-year-olds!' Weirdly, the group had lost to a rock band in their thirties. Nobody to this day seems quite sure how the categories worked …

Mathew was undeterred. In fact, he only became more determined. He left his salesman job, moved the family to a smaller house, and started his own company – Music World Management – to co-manage the group with Tillman. Girls Tyme, which had been trimmed down to a trio of Beyoncé, Kelly and LaTavia, now added another local girl, LeToya Luckett. It was decided that a change of name might bring a change of luck, so Girls Tyme went out of the window. In came Somethin' Fresh. Then, Cliché. Then, The Dolls. It was 1996 before Tina Knowles suggested the name Destiny. By that time, her eldest daughter was on the way to meeting hers …

2

# DESTINY'S CHILD RISE

**B**eyoncé and her young bandmates were certainly not shy of hard work. They actively enjoyed honing their skills, as well as being commendably determined. In later years some sceptics questioned whether the 'pushy parent' single-mindedness of Mathew and Tina Knowles meant that the girls missed out on a conventional childhood. Beyoncé has always ardently denied this, defending her dad: 'He's a great father and a great manager.' Vernell Jackson, a family friend and co-owner of Tina's salon, told *Rolling Stone* magazine: 'There was a lot of stuff they had to sacrifice, like the friendships they would have formed outside … but they were determined. People think that parents push their children, but Mathew and Tina weren't ever like that. They were more like: my daughter wants to do this, and it's the one thing she wants to do.' Mathew and Andretta Tillman supported the girls in the pursuit of their dreams and they wanted to give the girls the very best opportunity for success and so, during school vacations, they organized extra singing, dancing and aerobics classes.

By 1994 this dedication began to pay dividends. Tina Knowles had been reading the Bible – specifically, the Book of Isaiah – and saw the word 'Destiny': a light bulb went on. Under this name, the blend of raw talent and sleek sophistication that the four girls exhibited landed them their first record deal with Elektra Records the following year. Their new status saw the label securing them support slots for major artists who were playing in Houston. Destiny opened for hip-hop and R&B acts such as Dru Hill, Das EFX and girl band SWV, who offered helpful advice. 'They've been like big sisters to us,' remarked Beyoncé. She told the local press, 'They've talked to us about pacing ourselves, and watching out for people who could be hurtful to our careers.' Already, it seemed, there was something about the girls – their talent, unquestionably, but

# FAMILY *affair*

It's not only Beyoncé who kept it in the family when it came to management. Behind all of the stars featured here is a parent who helped pave the way to the top.

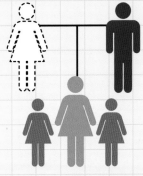

Beyoncé and Destiny's Child

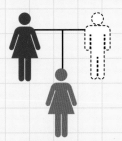

Jewel

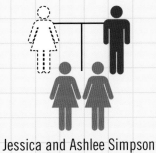

Jessica and Ashlee Simpson

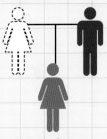

Justin Timberlake

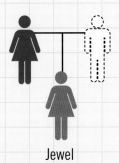

Miley Cyrus

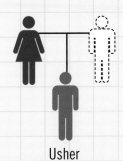

Usher

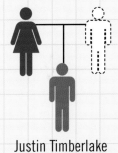

Britney Spears

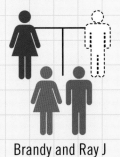

Brandy and Ray J

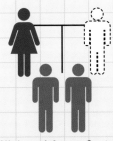

Nick and Aaron Carter

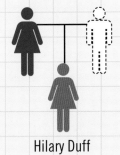

Hilary Duff

perhaps also their ambition and formidable work ethic, even at a young age – that helped them to attract the kind of mentorship most debut artists can only dream of. This would remain the case as the girls' careers blossomed and they continued to seek inspiration from those who had come before them.

One of their major influences was En Vogue, a hugely successful R&B act who went on to sell twenty million records. It was actually En Vogue's manager, Sylvia Rhone, who brought Destiny to the record label Elektra's attention in 1995, and the girls were thrilled to share a stable with their idols. 'Oh, they were our biggest,' Beyoncé told the *Washington Post*, years down the line. 'They all had their own individual looks, but they also looked like a group. They had wonderful routines but they also had great harmonies. Great songs, great routines … we would sit and watch them and pretend to be them.'

However, this record deal was to prove to be a learning curve rather than the big breakthrough they'd hoped for. Just a year on, citing them as 'too young and underdeveloped', Elektra dropped the girls. It must have been a crushing blow at the time, and indeed Beyoncé admitted as much. 'We thought the world was at an end,' she said in a later interview, though she soon took the lessons learned on board. While the label must have been kicking themselves since, Beyoncé

## 'WE WERE SO YOUNG, AND THERE'S ONLY SO MUCH YOU CAN SING ABOUT AT THAT AGE.'

has calmly reasoned that their decision was entirely understandable at that point. 'We did need more work back then,' she admitted. 'We weren't actually that good. We were SO young, and there's only so much you can sing about at that age.' The group needed more time to grow, and the girls – still only fourteen – needed to mature into the themes that would become the rallying cry of their later work.

Not to be knocked back, the dauntless Mathew took just a few weeks to secure another deal for them. Columbia Records, the noted Sony offshoot, took the plunge. Technically, Destiny were no more, having now tweaked their name to Destiny's Child. A fresh start beckoned, and the feel-good factor among the team was back, until a tragic event brought everyone down to earth. Andretta

**LEFT:** LeToya Luckett, Beyoncé, Kelly Rowland and LaTavia Roberson, pictured here in 1998, the year their debut album was released.

# THE CLOSER I GET *to you*

People who have influenced Destiny's Child have also worked with some of the industry's biggest names. Check out who has influenced who in the music biz.

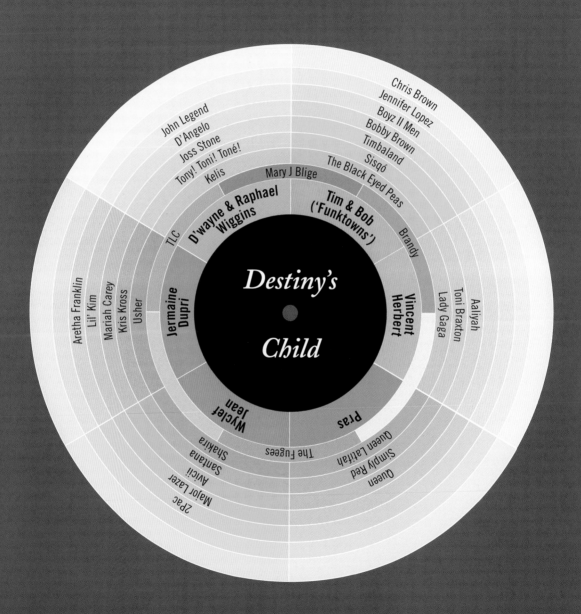

Tillman, the co-manager who had been so important in coaching the girls, passed away, a victim of the disease lupus. Andretta had brought Beyoncé and LaTavia together when the girls were only ten, and had been with them ever since. Having thought of her as an extra family member for a third of their lives, the girls were distraught.

They channelled their sorrow into their efforts, and emerged more determined than ever to make a success of their careers. In 1997 they began recording their first album. Beyoncé Knowles, Kelly Rowland, LaTavia Roberson and LeToya Luckett were only just turning sixteen, but already shared years of music industry experience. After seeing them perform a spontaneous showcase at the studio, the *Houston Chronicle*'s reporter proudly gushed: 'It was as if a quartet of angels descended from the heavens.' The girls put it more prosaically: 'We're very close to each other, like sisters. We're just four southern girls raised together in school and at church.'

They may still have been teenagers, but they knew what they wanted and how they wished to go about recording their debut. With Mathew now the full manager rather than co-manager, they didn't just hire an obvious seasoned producer to direct their sound. Instead, a host of names would ultimately be involved, with the first sessions taking place in California under the eyes and ears of the Wiggins brothers, otherwise known as two thirds of then-huge R&B trio Tony! Toni! Toné!

The debut single by Tony! Toni! Toné!, 'Little Walter', had topped the R&B charts in 1988. They'd gone on to have a run of hit albums and supported Beyoncé favourite Janet Jackson on a US stadium tour. Another aspect that appealed to the Knowleses was their close family bond: Dwayne and Raphael (born Charles Ray) Wiggins were joined in their trio by a cousin, Timothy Christian. They were also gospel-loving churchgoers. Dwayne, the chief writer and producer, had first heard Destiny's Child, he told an interviewer, a year or two earlier – on the phone after a friend in Houston had eulogized about the band, and played them to Wiggins down the line.

'I was just blown away,' he said. 'When I learned their ages, I just said, "Yeah, right." I figured anyone that good would already have a [record] deal, or that nobody that young would be able to blow like that.' By now they did have a deal of course, and, when Mathew Knowles got in touch with Wiggins, everybody was

## DESTINY'S *timeline*

It's hard to keep up with the changing members of Destiny's Child as the band scaled the charts but what's clear is that Queen Bey has been a constant shining star, driving the band on since they first found success

BEYONCÉ KNOWLES

MICHELLE WILLIAMS

FARRAH FRANKLIN

1995 1996 1997 1998 1999 2000 2001 2002 2003 2004 2005 2006

*Destiny's Child*

*8 Days of Christmas*

*Destiny Fulfilled*

*Survivor*

*The Writing's on the Wall*

Beyoncé Knowles

LaTavia Roberson

Nikki Taylor

Nina Taylor

Kelly Rowland

Támar Davis

LeToya Luckett

Michelle Williams

Farrah Franklin

LATAVIA ROBERSON

LETOYA LUCKETT

KELLY ROWLAND

enthusiastic for Destiny's Child to go to his studio in Oakland, in the San Francisco Bay Area, to start the serious part of their recording careers. Wiggins found them diligent and ambitious. 'I immediately knew that these girls were going to be huge,' he said. 'They were just like regular teenagers at times, laughing and playing, which was refreshing to see – but they took their work very seriously.' This was not to be the last time that Beyoncé's ferocious ability and motivation wowed people at the top end of the business. She would consistently dazzle and attract.

Here, as previously, these traits stood her in good stead in the studio. Wiggins was just one of a fleet of big names who were happy to help out. The hit-to-be 'No, No, No Part 1' was co-written and produced by Vincent Herbert, who had previously worked with Toni Braxton and Brandy. The gurus behind the success of Boyz II Men, Tim Kelley and Bob Robinson, offered up 'Tell Me'. And Jermaine Dupri, who's written and produced for everyone from Mariah Carey to Aretha Franklin and from TLC to Lil' Kim, and had at the time just finished work on Usher's second album, made his way to Oakland to produce and rap on 'With Me Part 1'.

Still more big names lined up to lend their support. The Fugees were one of the biggest soul/R&B acts of the Nineties, and, with their singer Lauryn Hill pregnant, Wyclef Jean and Pras, the two other members, had time to contribute. Wyclef was already branching out to an almost ubiquitous extent, and his solo debut was imminent. Nonetheless, he and Pras produced and rapped on the girls' 'Illusion', a revamping of British soul trio Imagination's slinky, underrated hit 'Just an Illusion', which had previously been released in 1982. There's an added piquancy to Beyoncé singing that opening line of 'Looking for a destiny that's mine …' She wasn't just name-checking half her band's moniker; she was testifying. She believed in that destiny. Wyclef also suggested a re-recording of 'No, No, No Part 1', which became, 'No, No, No Part 2'.

Elsewhere, on what became a diverse and eclectic album, there was a cover of The Commodores' golden oldie 'Sail On', which effectively demonstrated Beyoncé's multi-octave range and vocal dexterity. The girls knew this was their big shot, and were determined to display their versatility. They dedicated the album to 'our guardian angel', the late Andretta Tillman. A release date of February 1998 was set, which meant the quartet had a tantalizing and frustrating wait to see how it was received by the outside world.

Their first offering as a recording act was to come more promptly. Their track 'Killing Time', a Dwayne Wiggins creation, was promoted by Columbia on the *Men in Black* soundtrack. The Will Smith sci-fi comedy vehicle was one of 1997's biggest box-office hits, and the soundtrack album – also featuring names such as A Tribe Called Quest, Snoop Doggy Dogg (as he was then known), Ginuwine and Nas – was a Billboard number one. The girls were naturally thrilled at this auspicious opening gambit, and excited to be flown to New York for the launch party where they rubbed shoulders with the celebrity likes of Smith, Puff Daddy and Mary J. Blige.

Their profile was rising. 'Signing to Columbia was our turning point,' Beyoncé later recognized. 'We all knew it. So when it was time to make our

**ABOVE:** LaTavia Roberson, Beyoncé and Kelly Rowland performing in 1998, before the band split.

album, we never looked back. We were all so glad to finally have the opportunity that all of our past problems seemed to disappear.' If she sounds wise beyond her years, it's because at this point – two record deals in, and still only sixteen – she probably was.

Her appetite to play live was still growing and the girls adapted cheerily to their first experience of life on the road. Destiny's Child were now sent on tour as Wyclef's support act, and the Wyclef-assisted track 'No, No, No Part 2' became

Three Soul Train Lady of Soul Awards including Best New Artist for 'No, No, No'

Remix version of 'No, No, No' reached No. 1 on the Billboard Hot R&B/Hip-Hop Singles & Tracks

No. 1 on the Billboard Hot R&B/Hip-Hop Singles & Tracks

No. 3 on Billboard Hot 100

Over 1 million copies sold in the US

No. 14 on Billboard Top R&B/Hip-Hop Albums

Peaked at No. 67 on Billboard 200

Destiny's Child

1998

**A STAR IS** *born*

Destiny's Child's first album of the same name met with great success and heralded the arrival of a female force to be reckoned with.

their official debut single, released in October 1997. How would the girls be received outside of their comfort zone of Houston? Rather well, it transpired, as they wowed the arenas and earned the applause of Wyclef's crowds. The single was getting plenty of radio play across the States, and by the end of the year had soared into the Billboard chart's top three, reaching platinum status. (It later made the UK top five.) 'With Me' was released as a European single, and made it into the UK top twenty.

When *Destiny's Child*, the album, came out on 17 February 1998, they were mildly disappointed to find a hit single didn't automatically lead to a monster album. Sure, it did respectably well, and eventually – boosted by the megawatt superstardom to come – sold a million copies worldwide, but a Billboard chart peak of number sixty-seven felt like a letdown after the single's stirring success. It was an album of both peaks and padding, which is not uncommon for a new band working out their identity, whilst finding their strengths and weaknesses.

Some critics thought it wasn't different enough from the other female R&B/pop acts around. Others praised the harmonies, while a few seemed distracted by the leather dresses the quartet wore on the album cover. There wasn't so much a consensus as confusion. The more earnest noted that the combination of producers and cameo spots, as is the case on many an album in the genre, gave it a lack of overall cohesion. 'Their voices sound beautiful, but … indistinguishable from all the other female groups,' reckoned *All Music Guide*, while *NME* rather patronizingly decided: 'These are nice girls. Good girls.' *USA Today* declared: 'This quartet of Houston sixteen-year-olds debut with an album worthy of a more veteran act. Despite their youth, these women have been together for eight years, and their harmonies benefit from that familiarity on such sexy ballads as "Tell Me" and "Killing Time".'

Destiny's Child intelligently absorbed that it was an important first step on the ladder, and renewed their efforts. Touring and in-store signings continued as vital experience and promotion, and the girls supported popular Philadelphia soul group Boyz II Men across the States. Meanwhile, manager Mathew had seen how well the *Men in Black* tie-in track had done, and set the girls up with a track on the film *Why Do Fools Fall in Love*, a biopic of singer Frankie Lymon, a Fifties pop star who died tragically young. The real draw for the band, however, was that Missy Elliott and Timbaland were overseeing the soundtrack. Destiny's Child's credibility could only be enhanced from their association with such hot urban music producers. And when Missy and Timbaland co-wrote a song for the girls, called 'Get on the Bus', they were ecstatic to take a ride. Sonically it was a big leap forward for Destiny's Child too, with Beyoncé's vocals showcased. Beyoncé later revealed that while they – contrary, perhaps, to their ultra-confident image – were shy to meet their idol, Missy was even shyer than them at first: 'But she's so funny … we got really close to her, and love her so much.' The soundtrack album also featured En Vogue, and Missy duetting with Busta Rhymes. Now a go-to act for such contributions, Destiny's Child also sang a track for the Eddie Murphy movie *Life*. Produced by R. Kelly, 'Stimulate Me' starred on the soundtrack, which was co-produced by their pal Wyclef.

It was a remarkable roster of big-hit collaborators. If it seemed like Mathew Knowles' management techniques never made one false move, well, nobody's flawless. Seeking to raise their profile in the UK, he got them to sing backing vocals on a cover of Hall & Oates' 'She's Gone' by Matthew Marsden, an actor on the British soap opera *Coronation Street*. It was a minor hit in the UK, and all but invisible in the US. Today, Marsden may not have the same name recognition as Beyoncé, but he can always boast that she was once his backing singer.

In other long-ago moves, the girls' learning arc took in acting in the TV show *Smart Guy*, which aired to a largely teenage audience on The WB, a Warner Brothers-controlled station, and garnered respectable ratings. While it may not go down as a modern masterpiece, it did help generate exposure amongst the key youth demographic. It was also an early hint that Beyoncé would relish the big screen in later years. It would come to relish her too. Meanwhile, alongside their screen work, the group were winning their first awards: at the Soul Train Lady of Soul awards in September 1998, they won Best Album, Best Single and Best New Artists.

The year had busily rushed by, filled up with the promotion of their debut album. After touring around Europe, followed by a further six-week stint across the US with Jagged Edge and Jon B, the pressure was growing to record a follow-up album. Or, more accurately, to record a bumper-size 'hit' album. Their diaries were stuffed, though: in Britain alone they played eighteen concerts in seventeen days towards the tail end of 1998. However, their teenage hunger had not diminished.

So now it was time to get recording. The girls, whose work ethic was still electric, felt more experienced and sought more control over what they aimed for this time. Beyoncé told fans: 'During our first album, we made a list of mistakes, and we've made a list of changes for the second album. We knew we wanted a new sound and a new producer.' They also wanted to have more of a hand in the songwriting, and even the production. Putting their heads together with Mathew, they decided to first contact Kevin 'She'kspere' Briggs, a Timbaland acolyte whose name was in vogue after producing the global dance-floor hit 'No Scrubs' for TLC. With Destiny's Child keen to rest from their touring and record this album in Houston, he flew there, and work commenced.

Given the talent at play, it was inevitable that a big hit would result. Just a few days after meeting, they'd teamed up to pen the hit 'Bills, Bills, Bills'. Released as the lead single in June 1999, it was the group's first number one, both in the US and Canada. In America, where it knocked Jennifer Lopez's debut single 'If You Had My Love' off the top of the charts, it became the ninth-best selling single of the year. It also made the top ten in the UK and the top twenty in most of Europe. Two Grammy Award nominations ensued, for Best R&B Song and Best R&B Performance by a duo or group with vocals. And all this with a video shot in a beauty salon as a nod to Beyoncé's mother, Tina.

The song was the first flash of the 'independent women' motif, which was to become the group's, and later Beyoncé's, recurring calling card. Although co-written with the other girls and their producer, 'Bills, Bills, Bills' foreshadowed perennial lyrical themes that have been reiterated right through to 2016's *Lemonade*.

In 'Bills, Bills, Bills', influenced no doubt in part by the spirit of 'No Scrubs', Beyoncé berates an impecunious boyfriend in a relationship that has become increasingly one-sided. Here, as in later songs, Beyoncé treads a fine line between playing with ideas of traditional gender roles and a fierce call to arms for women

# DESTINY'S CHILD *vs* TLC

Both TLC and Destiny's Child had attitude and a multitude of hits between them, but listener data from Spotify reveals that it's Beyoncé's girls who achieved the most all-time streams and a higher proportion of monthly listeners tuning in to hear their catchy tracks.

— = 1,000,000 streams

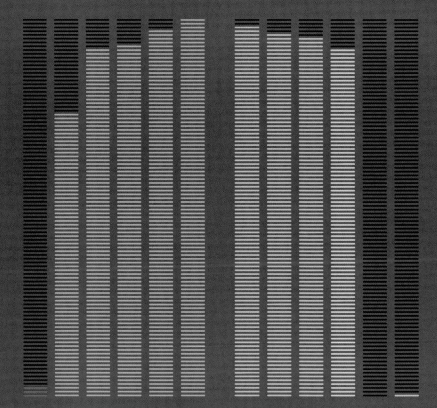

## DESTINY'S CHILD         TLC

| | | |
|---|---|---|
| — 382,660,968 | ALL TIME STREAMS | 289,110,497 — |
| — 75,335,805 – 'Say My Name' | MOST STREAMED SONG | 'No Scrubs' – 92,470,911 — |
| — 2,667,190 – 'So Good' | SONG DESERVING MORE STREAMS | 'Hat 2 Da Back' –796,769 — |

fed up with being taken advantage of. It's a masterful balancing act, though some were unable to see past lyrics that, on the surface, could be read as materialistic. As Tracie Egan Morrissey, writing for *Jezebel*, notes:

> Critics have been misinterpreting Beyoncé's overtly pro-woman lyrics as being anti-feminist ever since 1999's 'Bills, Bills, Bills'. Remember when people were all up in arms about the lyrics, 'Can you pay my bills? / Can you pay my telephone bills? / Can you pay my automo' bills?' thinking that they promoted the lifestyle of a kept woman? If you pay closer attention, you'll discover that the song is really about a deadbeat who is running up debt in his girlfriend's name.

Beyoncé needn't have worried that her fans would miss the message. They loved it. And LaTavia was very clear that the song had nothing to do with judging a man by the size of his wallet. 'People might say "Y'all are gold-diggers" when they hear it,' she said on the press release on the band's website. 'But it's totally different. It's about a relationship where the guy starts out nice, caring and considerate. Three or four months down the line, though, he starts slacking, borrowing your car, and when he gives it back to you, the tank is on empty. He'll use your cellphone and run it up, and buy you gifts with your own money. It's not a man-hating song though … We wrote about it because I myself have been through something similar … and a lot of friends have too.' Beyoncé's other bandmates were also eager to clarify this point. LeToya said, 'We ain't asking guys to straight out pay our rent or anything like that. We aren't saying that you shouldn't help each other out in a relationship. But don't start taking advantage of each other.' And fans felt the message spoke to them – 'Bills, Bills, Bills', like 'No Scrubs', had struck a major chord.

She'kspere again proved his poetic qualities on 'So Good' and 'Bug a Boo'. The latter was their follow-up hit, released in August that same year, and which brushed the US top thirty, with a video (directed by Darren Grant and featuring basketball ace Kobe Bryant and band-friend Wyclef Jean) that received a huge amount of airplay and kept pumping up the promo drive for the album. The track used interpolations from a track by soft-rock giants Toto, and, like 'Bills, Bills, Bills', took aim at would-be domineering, manipulative men. In it,

Beyoncé is set up as the object of obsessive, almost stalker-like male attention – 'I can't even go out with my girlfriends / Without you trackin' me down' – only to subvert the idea of the male gaze and male ownership entirely. 'So what, you bought a pair of shoes / What now, I guess you think I owe you?' Beyoncé sings, defiantly rejecting the idea that a woman 'owes' a man anything. The song sent a powerful message to fans

**RIGHT:** Destiny's Child pose for photographs backstage during *MTV's Spring Break* in Cancun, Mexico, 2000.

that they should feel empowered to push back against male demands.

Ultimately, 'Bug a Boo' wasn't quite as commercially successful as anticipated, but the third single from the album – 'Say My Name' – was to reach anthem status. For this song they'd hired another of the era's most on-the-nose writer-producers, Rodney Jerkins. His number 'The Boy Is Mine', sung by Brandy and Monica, had been 1998's biggest pop single. Collaborating with the group to create 'Say My Name', released in November, he helped the album gather a second wind sales-wise, and the song – another US chart-topper and a UK top three hit – went on to win two Grammys in 2001. However, it hadn't fallen from the sky. Indeed, there had been much work in the studio over the production techniques, with Beyoncé – again displaying preternatural confidence for her age – pointing out that Jerkins had rendered it too busy. It's clear that she was already becoming the band's de facto leader. And Jerkins reworked the mix until all parties agreed it was right. The lyrics dealt, again, with the perils of romantic relationships, with the girls accusing the song's bad boy of cheating with another woman, which is why he won't say our heroine's name down the phone line.

The band's lyrics were always emotionally fraught, but now, for the first time, cracks were beginning to show in Destiny's Child's own real-life relationships. Suddenly, as success and stardom embraced them, some of the joy was tempered with fresh challenges. December 1999 saw work pressure and conflicts start to chip away at their happiness.

Almost before the public had a chance to take it in, Destiny's Child had lost two members and added new ones. LaTavia and LeToya claimed that the family affair had grown lopsided. By the time the video for 'Say My Name' was released at the beginning of 2000 the pair had been replaced by Michelle Williams (a backing singer with Monica) and actor-singer Farrah Franklin. Franklin, too, was to leave after a few months, and so Destiny's Child soon became a trio. Although a settlement was ultimately reached among the original line-up, the fallouts within the band took their toll

'MOST PEOPLE DON'T REALIZE THAT WE HAVE DEDICATED OUR LIVES TO THIS. WE ARE PROOF THAT, WHATEVER YOU PUT YOUR MIND TO, YOU CAN ACHIEVE.'

on Beyoncé and Kelly, but the streamlined outfit was well positioned for the success that was to follow.

Their second album, *The Writing's on the Wall*, released in July 1999, may have been tied up in the break-up, but it was also their big breakthrough, and captured their original hunger for hits. 'Jumpin', Jumpin'' settled in as one of the most radio-played cuts of the following year. Again, the girls had been able to call on an impressive group of collaborators. Missy Elliott was a guest contributor to 'Confessions', and Dwayne Wiggins, the duke of the debut album, was back again, offering the slinky 'Temptation'. Overall the opus was a solid step forward, with genuinely impressive vocals fusing fluidly with the sound.

Although its highest chart position was number five, the album hovered in this region for months and in late 2001 was certified as eight times platinum. Sales for the album are now estimated at around six and a half million in the States alone and it's still rated as one of the best-selling R&B releases of all time.

The ongoing themes of how relationships should be conducted – with a 'commandment' before each track (e.g. 'thou shalt pay bills', 'thou shall not bug') – rang true once more with the group's female fans. 'We called the album *The Writing's on the Wall* because it spells out what will happen in a relationship if people treat each other a certain way,' said Beyoncé.

Beyoncé's dream had taken off like a rocket – and she knew it. On the verge of superstardom as the century turned, she asserted, 'Most people don't realize that we have dedicated our lives to this. We are proof that, whatever you put your mind to, you can achieve. This is just the start for us, believe me.'

# DESTINY
# AT THE TOP

As Beyoncé had stated, with the belief to match her bravado, the year 2000 marked just the beginning of her ascent to the top. The group had surmounted some tough obstacles and survived a testing year. Challenges only steeled her resolve, induced an increased maturity and honed her vision of what she wanted to achieve. She and Kelly were still just eighteen, and learned swiftly to adapt to Destiny's Child's personnel changes. They had a great new album out, which, Beyoncé felt, embodied much of the change they'd experienced in their personal lives over the preceding year. 'This represents us progressing from girls to young women,' she said of *The Writing's on the Wall*. 'We're still young, but we've seen quite a lot in the last year or so. We've travelled and matured personally.'

The experience they'd gained, and their graduation from rookies to seasoned but youthful stars, helped them to land a dream support slot: on the first tour in five years of their heroes, TLC. They could now handle the rigours and pressures of such a high-profile tour and performed with the energy of teenagers but coupled with the know-how of wiser heads. Audiences were enthralled, and the girls' confidence grew. So, when a February 2000 announcement of the split officially came, Beyoncé and Kelly, the latter turning nineteen that month, were united in facing firmly forward. 'We couldn't be more excited that Michelle and Farrah have joined us,' they said at the time. 'We're all really looking forward to the next phase of Destiny's Child.'

Certainly the initial signs were good. The new quartet appeared at the Grammys and Soul Train Awards, where fans were introduced to the new group members. LA-born Farrah, who had first met Destiny's Child as an extra in

**RIGHT:** Kelly, Farrah, Michelle and Beyoncé: the new line-up.

the music video for 'Bills, Bills, Bills', had a background of singing, acting and dancing. In marked contrast, Michelle hailed from Rockford, Illinois, and had grown up wanting to be an obstetrician. She'd got as far as enrolling at university as a medical student before meeting Destiny's Child when they gigged with Monica, for whom she was providing backing vocals. The four girls got on well, but the work schedule was undoubtedly a baptism of fire for the new members: a whirlwind of long rehearsals, travel and promotional commitments.

The family vibe around the unit was still strong. The Knowleses looked after Michelle, who brought an exuberance and spontaneity to the group. She confessed to 'experimenting' in her youth, 'always doing something I had no business doing'. Yet, despite some comically candid early interviews, she became a consummate professional, protective of her privacy. 'It takes time for her to warm up,' Beyoncé told interviewers, 'but she's very funny'.

In a bid to show solidarity and harmony within the group, MTV came to Houston to interview the new Destiny's Child line-up. Michelle and Farrah, new to the PR circuit, were relatively quiet, but Beyoncé was very clear that she felt entirely positive about the direction in which the group was moving. 'We are very blessed right now,' she beamed. 'We have the number one single and we're very grateful the fans are still standing by us. We've actually sold over a million records since the change.' She admitted that there had been communication problems, but Kelly painted a slightly more visceral picture: 'There was a lack of communication and loyalty on their part. It's like a sore that festers, and grows, and just gets worse. Then it becomes infected. And that's exactly what happened.'

Both Beyoncé and Kelly were strong in their defence of Mathew Knowles. He was a 'protector', they said. And certainly it appeared that divisions among the original line-up ran deeper than simple management issues. From Beyoncé and Kelly's point of view, the other girls had chosen not to provide creative input when invited to and had lapsed into a more mercenary attitude. 'It was no longer a passion and a love [for them],' said Beyoncé. 'It was more like a job.' For a girl who, from an early age, had been single-minded in the pursuit of her own creative vision, this must have been all but incomprehensible. She also understood that withstanding the pressures of the music industry required not only a shared passion, but also a united front. 'When you're a group, then you have to be a group,' she said. 'You can't be two and two. That can't work. Everyone has to work as one. That's why we're Destiny's Child, not Destiny's Children. We feel like we represent one.'

Beyoncé had worked hard for her gateway to success, and this represented the first real threat to not only her professional future, but also her family and friendships. Despite her calm exterior, she was rattled. 'When it happened, for two weeks I stayed in my room and didn't move. I felt like I couldn't breathe. I had a nervous breakdown, I couldn't believe it. It hurt so bad,' she said. Exhausting though it was, all the hubbub sent album sales soaring even higher and success prompted the group to keep looking to the future, rather than dwelling on what would prove to be minor speed bumps. 'We're happy that we're able to move on,' said Beyoncé. She was never in any doubt that the show had to go on.

If the split had been traumatic, the upside was that it inspired new songs, as the girls began writing again. They announced a significant autumn tour of the States supporting another A-list name, Christina Aguilera. Soon they were to begin recording 'Independent Women Part 1', which was to raise their success to a new level. Yet there was still one more hurdle to be negotiated.

Farrah was already showing signs of fatigue, telling one reporter, 'The worst thing is you get no privacy and you can't go out and have fun and get crazy because it'll end up in a tabloid somewhere. It's not a normal lifestyle.' Though she was clearly enjoying parts of the platform that celebrity provided – 'It's great to have the opportunity to meet people like Diana Ross,' she enthused – in another interview by MTV, en route to a show in Washington DC, she spoke of exhaustion and poor health. 'I have not slept in twenty-six hours. I went to hospital yesterday for dehydration and stomach flu … I'm just trying to get through this day.' She was clearly struggling, though she insisted gamely, 'I still can't wait to perform!'

It wasn't to be. She didn't make the gig, and on 19 July 2000, just five months after Farrah joined the group, a statement was released via their record label, Columbia: 'Destiny's Child and Farrah Franklin have parted ways. The group will continue as a trio for the time being with original members Beyoncé

> 'WHEN YOU'RE A GROUP, THEN YOU HAVE TO BE A GROUP… EVERYONE HAS TO WORK AS ONE. THAT'S WHY WE'RE DESTINY'S CHILD, NOT DESTINY'S CHILDREN.'

Knowles and Kelly Rowland and new member Michelle Williams.' Media interest, understandably, was high, but Beyoncé and Kelly were clear: 'Farrah was NOT kicked out,' Beyoncé told Carson Daly on MTV. Rather, it seemed, Farrah had struggled under the heavy demands of being a member of one of the world's fastest-rising and hardest-working acts, and already she'd missed several events. As Beyoncé noted, 'We also had a five-day promotional trip to Australia and she didn't come. So we all agreed that we should part ways. It was a group decision, not a management decision.' She was confident that the trio would shine on the Christina Aguilera tour: 'I know that we get all of our energy from the crowd, and we've definitely been getting that and more.'

Such energy was a pre-requisite to maintaining the level of work and degree of flair that made Destiny's Child the success that they were. Kelly clearly thought so, criticizing Franklin for what she saw as standing up their fans – 'something Destiny's Child does not do'. Michelle added that she thought Farrah 'couldn't handle the stress, and the work that comes with this'.

From the struggle came forth sweetness. Now the 'classic' line-up was finally in place. The Aguilera tour commenced, and soon the girls were called on to demonstrate that stamina and determination which was key to life in Destiny's Child. If you fell, you got back up again. Kelly did indeed fall, literally, backstage during a rushed costume change at a Denver arena. She broke two toes in her right foot – but the tour, nonetheless, went on. Kelly wasn't going to 'stand up' the fans, but she did sit down for them, performing perched on a stool. And Beyoncé's sister, Solange, now aged fourteen – and with a debut album of her own out soon – took over Kelly's choreography onstage.

With such a can-do attitude, the future looked bright. Their new track, 'Independent Women Part 1', recorded in New York and at SugarHill Studios in Houston, was to propel them onto the next plane of superstardom. Their first solid gold classic had come through an unanticipated channel. They'd been invited to come up with a song for the blockbuster movie *Charlie's Angels* starring Cameron Diaz, Drew Barrymore and Lucy Liu, a revamp of the much-loved and splendidly cheesy Seventies TV show. 'I got a chance to actually write and produce the song,' grinned a justifiably proud Beyoncé. 'When the label heard it, they were like: "This is hot!"' It was scorching. Indeed, Beyoncé would go on to play a major role in the writing and production of the entire album. This is where

# DESTINY *under cover*

No one has covered Destiny's Child tracks more than Beyoncé. Catchy, upbeat and empowering, Destiny's Child songs capture the imaginations of other musicians, as well as their fans. This graph shows the six artists who have covered the most Destiny's Child tracks, as well as the number of times they have performed a Destiny's Child song.

They Might Be Giants **57**

Fifth Harmony **53**

Kelly Rowland **15**

Rita Ora **10**

Michelle Williams **5**

**Beyoncé
2,049**

her thoughts, her ideas, her personality and attitudes began to strongly show through her music.

'Independent Women Part 1' was released in October 2000, and all the line-up changes – even though it was the first and last track with both Farrah and Michelle on vocals – were instantly consigned to history. It wowed the world. It spent no less than eleven weeks on top of the Billboard chart, from November 2000 right through to January 2001, thus technically being number one in two different centuries! The *Charlie's Angels* soundtrack also sold a million and a half copies, chiefly on the

appeal of this single, whose LA-shot video tied in with the movie. The Grammy-nominated track was also a massive number one in Canada, New Zealand, the Netherlands and the UK. As icing on the cake, Destiny's Child won Soul Train's prestigious Sammy Davis Jr Entertainer of the Year Award for 2000.

Yet it wasn't just the song's commercial reach and skittering counter-intuitive rhythms that impressed. Its witty lyrics (with shout-outs to the 'Angels') and feisty stance made a striking and resonant cultural impact too. As with the group's previous hit singles, this track looked at the balance of power within romantic relationships, and this time was overt in advocating 'always 50/50'. If some critics had missed the point with 'Bills, Bills, Bills', Beyoncé was going to make sure that they got the message this time. 'Pay my own fun, oh, and I pay my own bills,' she sang. The song was a powerful celebration of women who stand on their own two feet, buy their own

**RIGHT:** The four women singing their hearts out in 2000, at the Music Factory Awards in the Netherlands.

# SURVIVOR
## *statistics*

'Survivor' was a massive success story for Destiny's Child and became a hit single across the globe. But where in the world did the song resonate most with Beyoncé fans and how did it measure up in the charts?

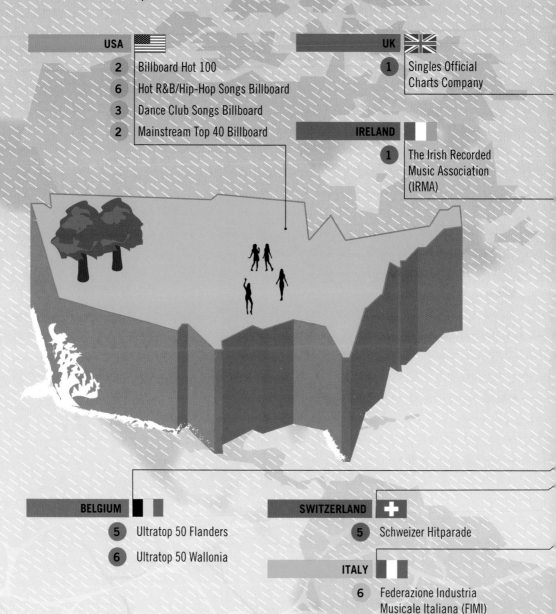

| USA | |
|---|---|
| 2 | Billboard Hot 100 |
| 6 | Hot R&B/Hip-Hop Songs Billboard |
| 3 | Dance Club Songs Billboard |
| 2 | Mainstream Top 40 Billboard |

| UK | |
|---|---|
| 1 | Singles Official Charts Company |

| IRELAND | |
|---|---|
| 1 | The Irish Recorded Music Association (IRMA) |

| BELGIUM | |
|---|---|
| 5 | Ultratop 50 Flanders |
| 6 | Ultratop 50 Wallonia |

| SWITZERLAND | |
|---|---|
| 5 | Schweizer Hitparade |

| ITALY | |
|---|---|
| 6 | Federazione Industria Musicale Italiana (FIMI) |

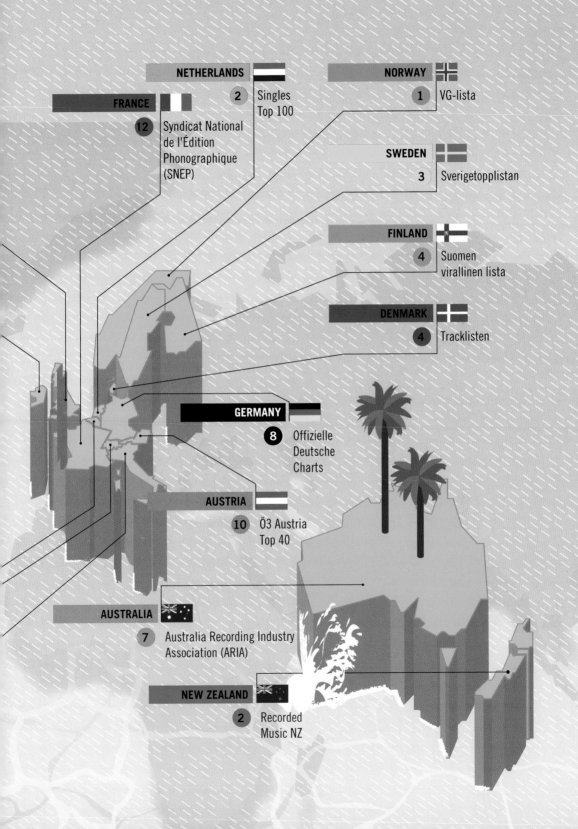

NETHERLANDS
2 · Singles Top 100

NORWAY
1 · VG-lista

FRANCE
12 · Syndicat National de l'Édition Phonographique (SNEP)

SWEDEN
3 · Sverigetopplistan

FINLAND
4 · Suomen virallinen lista

DENMARK
4 · Tracklisten

GERMANY
8 · Offizielle Deutsche Charts

AUSTRIA
10 · Ö3 Austria Top 40

AUSTRALIA
7 · Australia Recording Industry Association (ARIA)

NEW ZEALAND
2 · Recorded Music NZ

clothes, house and car, and could proclaim, with their idol, 'I depend on me.' When Beyoncé exhorted her fans – 'all the honeys who makin' money' – to 'throw your hands up at me', a new anthem was born.

However, before its momentum could lead into the new album – and new millennium – the group needed closure. Legal matters with the departing ex-members had to be resolved: such things are always convoluted, and cross words were exchanged.

It was tricky for Beyoncé, who was already perceived as very much the front person. She had been emotionally bruised, not only by the split of the original line-up and Farrah's subsequent departure, but also by the accusations in some camps that Mathew favoured her over other band members. 'Sometimes I wish my father wasn't the manager,' she told *Vibe* in a candid interview in February 2001 that hints at the fatigue she must have been feeling at this point.

> Then people might stop attacking me. Whenever something goes wrong in the group, it's my fault. Blame Beyoncé. Somebody left the group, it's Beyoncé's fault. Kelly broke her toes, it's Beyoncé's fault. I have to be extra tight and prove myself every day. It's really unfair because nobody else has to do that. It's not Sisqó's fault when he sings lead. It's not Coko's fault that she sang lead. The haters make me feel bad about singing lead, when that should be something that I'm happy about.

And there was plenty to feel happy about. In February 2001, the group won two of their five Grammy nominations for 'Say My Name'. Beyoncé was thrilled. 'It's something most people wait their whole career to accomplish. We were so shocked.' The very next evening, Destiny's Child appeared at a concert at the White House, along with Jessica Simpson, Ricky Martin and 98 Degrees. It was the first time Beyoncé would play for a sitting president, and, whatever her politics, she must still have felt the considerable honour.

It was time to drop the record. The third – and probably the definitive – Destiny's Child album, *Survivor*, was released by Columbia on 1 May 2001. Beyoncé was listed as one of the prime producers, with others including Anthony Dent, Rob Fusari, Poke & Tone and Cory Rooney. Dwayne Wiggins continued to be involved, too. *Survivor* went on to sell over ten million copies worldwide, with almost half of that number in the States. It went straight in at number one on the Billboard charts, received three Grammy nominations, was certified quadruple platinum within a year and spawned five hit singles, three of which – 'Independent Women Part 1', 'Survivor' and 'Bootylicious' – have indisputably attained pop classic status.

The album title and theme had come indirectly from the group's internal problems, as Beyoncé wryly admitted. 'I heard this DJ on the radio saying Destiny's Child was like the *Survivor* television show: you had to guess which member would be out next. So I thought I'd take that and turn it into a positive thing.' There is a strong sense that Beyoncé was the guiding force behind this album, though she modestly claimed that her co-writing and co-producing all the tracks had come about by accident as much as design. 'I only wanted to do, like, three songs,' she said. 'The label kept saying do another one, do another song, do another song … It wasn't planned.' She also pointed out that on *Survivor* 'everyone sang leads. On the last album I sang most of the leads because the producers told me to. It was important to me that Kelly and Michelle sang leads on this album, because they are so musically strong.'

The album launched at a New York party where guests included Eve, Joe, Bilal and most notably one Jay-Z, about whom we'll be hearing much more later, with those in attendance witnessing Destiny's Child being carried on stage by musclemen in combat gear. As their highest-charting album, it soon went to number one across the US, Canada and most of Europe, too.

The video for the song 'Survivor' shows the girls shipwrecked on a desert island, but resilient and invincible – like superheroes. In what retrospectively looks like a last stand by the previous generation, the track was kept from number one in the States by Janet Jackson's 'All for You'. But there could be no doubt that Destiny's Child – and their fans – felt the future was theirs. The song celebrated the band's refusal to lie down and their determination to push through whatever might come their way: 'Now that

**NEXT PAGE:** Beyoncé, Kelly and Michelle at the 2001 Billboard Music Awards, after winning Artist of the Year.

# KEEP ON *surviving*

This graphic shows the number of times different members of Destiny's Child have performed 'Survivor' live including dates of first and latest performances by each artist.

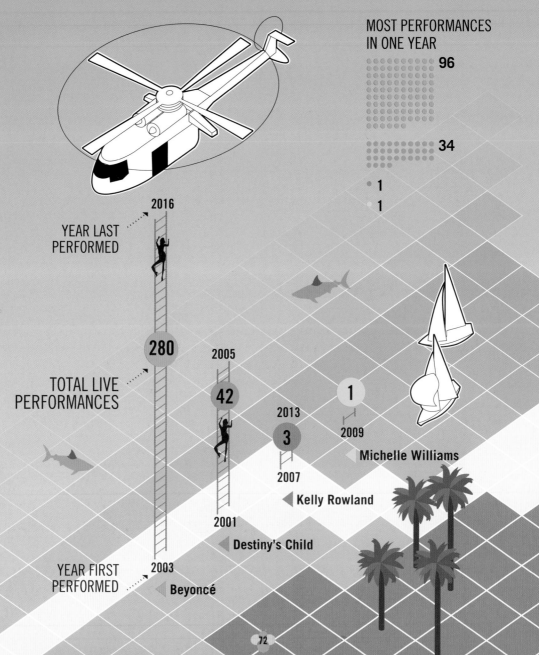

MOST PERFORMANCES
IN ONE YEAR

96

34

1

1

YEAR LAST
PERFORMED

2016

280

TOTAL LIVE
PERFORMANCES

2005

42

2013

3

1

2009

2007

Michelle Williams

Kelly Rowland

2001

Destiny's Child

YEAR FIRST
PERFORMED

2003

Beyoncé

you're out of my life I'm so much better / You thought that I'd be broke without you, but I'm richer.' Listeners loved the sterling show of strength and the song rapidly became an 'I Will Survive' for the twenty-first century.

It was, of course, possible to interpret the song as a dig at former bandmates, but Kelly Rowland emphasized that the lyrics had broader meaning: 'Everyone thinks the song is directed at them, but it's actually just a song for anyone who's been through a survivor situation.' Beyoncé was more precise. 'The lyrics ... are Destiny's Child's story, because we've been through a lot. We went through our dramas with the members and everybody was like, "Oh well, no more Destiny's Child." Well, we sold even more records after all of the changes. Any complications we've had in our ten-year period of time have made us closer and tighter and better.' She wasn't afraid to acknowledge the tough times, but nor was she going to let them defeat her.

> 'EVERYONE THINKS THE SONG IS DIRECTED AT THEM, BUT IT'S ACTUALLY JUST A SONG FOR ANYONE WHO'S BEEN THROUGH A SURVIVOR SITUATION.'

The next big hit from the album drew inspiration from another female icon. Beyoncé said she was listening to Stevie Nicks' 'Edge of Seventeen' on a flight when the topline of 'Bootylicious' came to her. Co-writer and co-producer Rob Fusari, who went on to work with everyone from Lady Gaga to ABC, later recalled the seeds of the track slightly differently, saying that they weren't able to use the first choice, the guitar riff from the band Survivor's rock chestnut 'Eye of the Tiger', and so adopted the fairly similar 'Edge of Seventeen'.

Were the public ready for this jelly? Undoubtedly. 'Bootylicious' was good, honest fun – in Michelle's words, 'If you've got a big booty, it's OK. Just put on some pants and be confident.' Another track on the album, 'Nasty Girl', explored the flip side of female sexuality. Celebrating yourself as an independent woman was something to be encouraged, but Beyoncé was clear that there was a difference between confidence and classlessness. She was still, at heart, the Methodist girl who emphatically disapproved of 'Booty all out, tongue out her mouth, cleavage from here to Mexico'. Here, perhaps, we see the pressures of operating in an industry that insists its female stars are sexy, but not sleazy. Professionally, as well as personally, the 'around the block girls', Beyoncé sang,

# BOOTYLICIOUS

Destiny's Child's signature moves for the 'Bootylicious' video are some of their most fun and memorable and Queen Bey led the dance, swinging her hips and shaking her 'jelly' for her fans. Here is what is takes to create such a catchy number.

23   10   1

JELLY   BOOTYLICIOUS   VIBEALACIOUS

23
22
21
20
19
18
17
16
15
14
13
12
11
10
9
8
7
6
5
4
3
2
1
0

number of repetitions of the word in the song

make it 'hard for women like me who try to have some integrity / You make it hard for girls like myself who respect themselves / And have dignity'.

Outside the song's lyrics, Beyoncé clarified her stance further: 'Destiny's Child do not talk about sex in their lyrics,' she insisted. 'We do not promote sex and we do not go out of our way to be sexy. We will show skin but we have to feel comfortable.' Given the trends of the time, her thoughts were apposite. It was an era where female stars were becoming – or being pushed to become – raunchier by the minute, with Britney Spears' 'I'm a Slave 4 U' and Christina Aguilera's 'Dirrty' employing more-than-suggestive lyrics and lascivious videos. (Miley Cyrus' shock tactics were a way off, but the door was opened.) Some said such untethered overt sexuality was feminist; others thought young women were being coerced by male music industry heads. Still others, like journalist James Dickerson, believed that female stars like Beyoncé had perfected the formula for success: music that 'expressed male fantasies about women', yet carried rebellious messages that struck a chord with female listeners. Beyoncé herself was adamant that 'You can walk in somewhere in a nice sexy dress, but you carry yourself like a lady and have God with you.' God, it seems, was on her side.

> 'WE DO NOT PROMOTE SEX AND WE DO NOT GO OUT OF OUR WAY TO BE SEXY. WE WILL SHOW SKIN BUT WE HAVE TO FEEL COMFORTABLE.'

4

# BEYONCÉ GOES SOLO

**W**hile Destiny's Child were bringing something fresh to the R&B/pop crossover arena, they were also honouring the tradition of girl groups making strong points about the way women deserve to be treated. Respect was paramount in their ideology. In the *New York Times*, Ann Powers hailed them as the latest in a long line of female artists unafraid to promote female empowerment. 'As America's reigning girl group,' she wrote, 'Destiny's Child is in the thick of a post-feminine revolution. From The Shirelles to TLC, girl groups have helped women hash out the differences between good and bad, liberation and entrapment, love and dependency. Since hip-hop's rise, girl groups have grown even tougher. Beyoncé Knowles, Kelly Rowland and Michelle Williams take on the predicaments of womanhood with the determination of warriors.'

*Survivor* continued to rack up the awards: among them, the American Music Award for Favorite Pop/Rock Album and the Teen Choice Award for R&B/Soul Album of the Year. Influential magazines considered them THE great pop group of the moment, dominating radio with liquid harmonies and inventive techno beats and remixes.

Beyoncé acknowledged the album's global sway, recognizing its success as 'very flattering, but it's very strange to us'. They were still, she insisted, 'just some Southern chicken-and-fry eating girls'. These no-frills girls were now being signed to massive marketing deals. They signed a footwear deal with Candies, and Beyoncé became a face of L'Oréal.

She also made baby steps into the acting and film world, playing the lead opposite Mekhi Phifer in MTV's 2001 production of *Carmen: A Hip Hopera*, a modern-day adaptation of Bizet's opera *Carmen*, set in Philadelphia and LA. Wyclef Jean, Jermaine Dupri, Mos Def and Rah Digga were among the cast. Beyoncé played a seductive aspiring actress, with whom Phifer's sergeant

**RIGHT:** Beyoncé on the day the album *Survivor* was released during 'hip-hop week' at the MTV studios.

becomes infatuated. Robert Townsend directed the film, inspired by the 1954 interpretation of the same opera, *Carmen Jones*. *Variety* praised Beyoncé's performance, in a foretaste of the silver screen success that would be hers in later life: 'Knowles makes a fine acting debut, and once again makes it clear that she's got a surplus of star power.'

The year continued to provide a curious mix of triumph and turmoil. After the tragedy of the 9/11 attacks, the group's European tour was cancelled and they instead appeared in two benefit concerts for the survivors of the attacks. Their own anthem of survival rang with an additional empowering layer of meaning.

**ABOVE:** The three girls perform at the Rockefeller Center in 2001.

After touring the States with Nelly and Eve, Destiny's Child's Christmas album came out well ahead of the day itself, in October. *8 Days of Christmas* included seasonal classics such as 'White Christmas', 'Silent Night' and 'Little Drummer Boy' (with Beyoncé's sister, Solange, guesting on that one). It peaked at number thirty-four in the US charts and sold half a million copies, with Beyoncé given writing credit on the new song that served as the title track. The trio were now mainstream, crossover superstars.

Solange herself was forging her own career, and the girls were happy to help, singing backing vocals on her theme for Disney's animated sitcom *The Proud Family*. In March 2002 a remix album of their best-loved tracks – titled *This is the Remix* – kept the group's name in the top twenty. The album wasn't perfect, but it included some inspired and radical remixes; Wyclef Jean, The Neptunes, Timbaland, Maurice Joshua and Missy Elliott were all involved.

The key moment of this period, even if its true importance only became obvious later, was when the three announced that they'd all be pursuing individual side projects, including solo albums. This was not, the girls were clear, as a result of any internal issues. Destiny's Child would continue just as dedicatedly as ever, they insisted, but a brief hiatus would be taken. Some thought Mathew was lining Beyoncé up for a solo breakaway, just as Berry Gordy Jr had nurtured Diana Ross' career post-Supremes. (Ironically this theory would be played out in later years when Beyoncé starred in the *Dreamgirls* movie.) Ultimately, she would achieve a peerless level of solo stardom, but for the time being she was content to bide her time, as it was Kelly and Michelle's solo projects that gave the girls their first glimpse of success outside of Destiny's Child.

First out of the blocks came Michelle Williams' debut, a contemporary gospel album titled *Heart to Yours*. It raced to the top of the Billboard gospel chart, the same week as the group published their autobiography, *Soul Survivors*. It was also 2002's biggest gospel album, with over 200,000 sales. William Ruhlmann from *AllMusic* described her voice in slightly patronizing terms, as 'warm and kittenish', though he went on to note that later in the album she transformed herself 'from kitten to tiger'. To this day, Michelle is a big name on the gospel circuit.

Then came Kelly's solo venture, which made an even bigger splash. Her guest vocal on Nelly's 'Dilemma' was one of 2002's biggest singles around the world, selling almost eight million copies and winning the duo a Grammy for Best Rap/Sung Collaboration. As the *Guardian*'s Caroline Sullivan pointed out, 'Rowland is no longer a mere backing vocalist for Beyoncé.'

Her solo album *Simply Deep*, recorded in just three weeks, emerged in October and surprised some with its higher-than-expected levels of experimentation and edginess. Solange and Brandy were among the backing vocalists while producers included Mark J. Feist, Big Bert and Rich Harrison. Kelly called it 'a weird fusion of a little bit of Sade and a little bit of rock'. Although 'Dilemma' was not the lead single for this album, it was released before the rest of the album was recorded and became the big hit. 'Stole' and 'Can't Nobody' were both released as supporting singles and performed reasonably well, the former reaching the top thirty in the US and both making the UK top five. The album went gold, and has to date sold just over half a million copies in the States and – thanks to a huge international reach, especially in the UK where it hit the number one spot – two and a half million copies worldwide.

Not everyone was entirely convinced. A contemporary review in *Entertainment Weekly* felt the album lacked oomph, with Jon Caramanica writing that Kelly's 'first solo project doesn't pull her out from Beyoncé's shadow. She needs added star power … her back-up singer instincts leave even the hottest songs here feeling somewhat chilly.' Regardless, the public had decided they were hot for Kelly, who now also moved into acting (hammy horror flick *Freddy vs Jason* was a box-office smash). And the worldwide success of 'Dilemma', and the subsequent earlier-than-planned release of *Simply Deep* to ride on this runaway popularity, meant that Kelly became the first member of Destiny's Child to have a number one hit outside the group.

Consequently, in response to Kelly's success, Beyoncé's solo debut had to be postponed more than once. There may or may not have been some nails chewed as she wondered if, in the fickle pop-culture world, a window of opportunity was closing. But Beyoncé had been far from idle while Kelly enjoyed her time in the sun. She was increasingly willing to demonstrate her own business acumen and strong marketing instincts, pragmatically telling *Newsweek* that she'd come to view the group's difficulties from the previous year as a positive, in business terms at least. 'Destiny's Child was always very talented, but I think the thing we were lacking was controversy,' she said. 'I think in order for your group to be successful, your story has to be interesting. Our story was very clean, so I thank God for the controversy. I'm happy because it helps me sell records.' And selling records was a skill that she was about to demonstrate, yet again, she had well and truly mastered.

Even before her solo debut she'd co-starred as Foxxy Cleopatra in the 2002 summer blockbuster comedy *Austin Powers in Goldmember*. The Mike Myers-led spy spoof saw Austin time-travelling to the Seventies to be reunited with his ex-lover Foxxy, who was working undercover as a disco singer. Foxxy's role demanded sex appeal and broad laughs, affectionately parodying Blaxploitation heroines such as Foxy Brown and Cleopatra Jones. Beyoncé performed with aplomb – it takes a certain swagger to deliver lines like, 'You're under arrest, sugah!' – and the film took around $300 million at the box office.

The soundtrack also featured Beyoncé's debut solo hit, 'Work It Out', her first collaboration with rising stars Pharrell Williams and Chad Hugo, the writing-production duo also known as The Neptunes, who would go on to dominate the music industry. With its nods to retro-funk stylings and hints of James Brown and Tina Turner, the song played up to the Foxxy Cleopatra identity, while showcasing Knowles' vocal chops. (It was intended as the opening track on

**ABOVE:** Kelly Rowland finding her feet as a solo artist, performing at the 8th Annual Soul Train Lady of Soul awards with Nelly.

# HIT ALBUM: *Dangerously in Love*

Breaking free from the restraints of Destiny's Child, Beyoncé's first solo album
smashed the charts and won awards all over the world for its numerous hit singles.

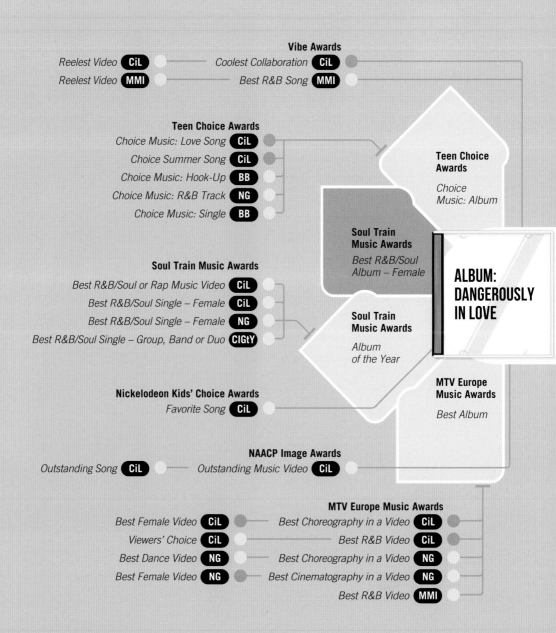

**Vibe Awards**

Reelest Video **CiL**     Coolest Collaboration **CiL**

Reelest Video **MMI**     Best R&B Song **MMI**

**Teen Choice Awards**

Choice Music: Love Song **CiL**

Choice Summer Song **CiL**

Choice Music: Hook-Up **BB**

Choice Music: R&B Track **NG**

Choice Music: Single **BB**

**Teen Choice Awards**

*Choice Music: Album*

**Soul Train Music Awards**

Best R&B/Soul or Rap Music Video **CiL**

Best R&B/Soul Single – Female **CiL**

Best R&B/Soul Single – Female **NG**

Best R&B/Soul Single – Group, Band or Duo **CIGtY**

**Soul Train Music Awards**

*Best R&B/Soul Album – Female*

**Soul Train Music Awards**

*Album of the Year*

**ALBUM: DANGEROUSLY IN LOVE**

**MTV Europe Music Awards**

*Best Album*

**Nickelodeon Kids' Choice Awards**

Favorite Song **CiL**

**NAACP Image Awards**

Outstanding Song **CiL**     Outstanding Music Video **CiL**

**MTV Europe Music Awards**

Best Female Video **CiL**     Best Choreography in a Video **CiL**

Viewers' Choice **CiL**     Best R&B Video **CiL**

Best Dance Video **NG**     Best Choreography in a Video **NG**

Best Female Video **NG**     Best Cinematography in a Video **NG**

Best R&B Video **MMI**

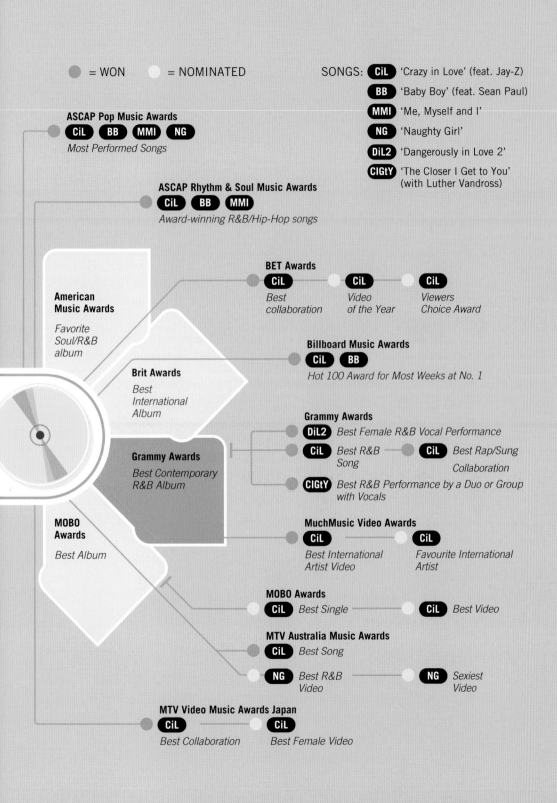

● = WON   ○ = NOMINATED

SONGS:
**CiL** 'Crazy in Love' (feat. Jay-Z)
**BB** 'Baby Boy' (feat. Sean Paul)
**MMI** 'Me, Myself and I'
**NG** 'Naughty Girl'
**DiL2** 'Dangerously in Love 2'
**CIGtY** 'The Closer I Get to You' (with Luther Vandross)

**ASCAP Pop Music Awards**
**CiL**   **BB**   **MMI**   **NG**
*Most Performed Songs*

**ASCAP Rhythm & Soul Music Awards**
**CiL**   **BB**   **MMI**
*Award-winning R&B/Hip-Hop songs*

**BET Awards**
**CiL** *Best collaboration*   **CiL** *Video of the Year*   **CiL** *Viewers Choice Award*

**American Music Awards**
*Favorite Soul/R&B album*

**Billboard Music Awards**
**CiL**   **BB**
*Hot 100 Award for Most Weeks at No. 1*

**Brit Awards**
*Best International Album*

**Grammy Awards**
**DiL2** *Best Female R&B Vocal Performance*
**CiL** *Best R&B Song*   **CiL** *Best Rap/Sung Collaboration*
**CIGtY** *Best R&B Performance by a Duo or Group with Vocals*

**Grammy Awards**
*Best Contemporary R&B Album*

**MuchMusic Video Awards**
**CiL** *Best International Artist Video*   **CiL** *Favourite International Artist*

**MOBO Awards**
*Best Album*

**MOBO Awards**
**CiL** *Best Single*   **CiL** *Best Video*

**MTV Australia Music Awards**
**CiL** *Best Song*
**NG** *Best R&B Video*   **NG** *Sexiest Video*

**MTV Video Music Awards Japan**
**CiL** *Best Collaboration*   **CiL** *Best Female Video*

her album, but then something bigger came along.) *Flak* magazine reckoned she sounded 'like Pam Grier taking five from the revolution to let her afro down'. As for the video, it got *PopMatters* rather heated: '[It] emphasizes Beyoncé's frankly awesome power, recalling Aretha and especially Tina as she snuggles up to the mic stand, her ferocious thighs revealed beneath a sequinned mini-skirt. In her first solo effort, Beyoncé declares herself a singular personality, a body, and a performer – not to mention a sensation with a hula-hoop.'

It was beginning to look as though the other Destiny's Child solo spinoffs were merely opening acts. Swiftly, Beyoncé had another film in the bag, as the musical comedy-drama *The Fighting Temptations* was shot, though release was held back until her album sent her supernova. In fact, a smaller-scale yet more telling and culturally resonant shoot took place around the same time, when she appeared in the video for Jay-Z's single '03 Bonnie & Clyde', on which she sang as Jay-Z rapped. The lead single from Jay-Z's seventh album *The Blueprint 2: The Gift & The Curse*, which has now sold over two million copies, was produced by one Kanye West, who at the time was not yet a household name. Released in October 2002, the track raced to number four in the US charts.

Perhaps more significantly, it repositioned Beyoncé, rebooting her image in the public's imagination around six months before her solo album. The video for '03 Bonnie & Clyde', directed by Chris Robinson and filmed in Mexico in November, cleverly and skilfully presented the 'new' Beyoncé as one possessed of a streetwise, in-your-face, devil-may-care attitude. It played on both the 1993 film *True Romance* and the timeless mythology of lovers on the run from the law, Bonnie and Clyde. As such, the video also suggested that Beyoncé was slightly less clean-cut than the persona she'd projected thus far. Not least because it seemed to hint that she and Jay-Z were rather familiar with each other outside a purely professional context …

The couple were now rumoured to be an item, 'Dangerously in Love' – and the video only furthered fervent speculation as to whether Beyoncé and Jay-Z were a real-life couple. And Beyoncé was having fun fanning the flames. She would go on to include the track as a bonus on international editions of her own album, crooning 'down to ride to the very end, me and my boyfriend', in a number that also saw her quoting lines from Prince's 'If I Was Your Girlfriend'. The rumours, it seemed, were true.

The effect of their personal relationship on their public profiles was enormous. In one easy move she and Jay-Z all but merged their huge audiences, giving her the credibility of a 'bad girl' edge and introducing his 'bad boy' music to a crossover crowd. It was a welcome expansion, and Beyoncé would continue

**ABOVE:** Beyoncé and the girls at the premiere of *Austin Powers in Goldmember* in 2002.

to embrace it, performing the song live for many years to come. In 2011 she introduced it onstage by confessing, 'It's 2002 … I started to feel a little lonely, until one day …' And on her and her now-husband's joint On the Run Tour of 2014, they opened the show with it. Safe to assume, then, that it's 'their tune' and the moment that soundtracked the beginning of their relationship.

The heat sparked by their romance would become a steadily burning blaze. In this moment, though, Beyoncé was about to have her own white-hot explosion. Her album, *Dangerously in Love*, was finally ready to drop and was released in June 2003. It would go on to dominate the charts that summer and beyond. Multi-platinum, it's now sold over eleven million copies, winning countless awards in the process. With Michelle Williams going gospel on her solo outing and Kelly Rowland going relatively 'alternative' on hers, Beyoncé instead focused firmly on R&B, dance and soul. It was a well-thought-out but nonetheless exciting balance of up-tempo club tracks, ballads and – as the singer put it herself – 'really sexy songs and songs that make you feel emotional … it's a nice mixture'.

Beyoncé had met with and interviewed several potential producers, initially working in Miami, Florida, with name-of-the-moment Scott Storch. Storch, who had been a member of The Roots, worked with Dr. Dre, 50 Cent, Snoop Dogg and Christina Aguilera. He was as hot as the sun in the business, and Beyoncé was savvy enough to spot it. She even moved into a Miami hotel for several months. But she was prolifically coming up with ideas for melodies and lyrics herself, and unsurprisingly the album ultimately boasted an array of producers, with Beyoncé claiming many writing and production credits. She shared the title of 'executive producer' with her father.

'Liberating and therapeutic' were the adjectives she used to describe recording without her bandmates, saying she felt more creatively herself. More confident daily, she contacted Missy Elliott, Sean Paul, Big Boi and even Luther Vandross for collaborations. And, of course, she didn't have to reach too far to get a Jay-Z guest appearance.

'Dangerously in Love 2' was a previously unheralded song she'd penned for the *Survivor* album: here, it acted as a tantalizing clue for her fans about events in her own love life. The delay in releasing the album, imposed by the success of Kelly's, became an advantage, giving her time to tweak and finesse her work, recording many more songs than made the final cut. 'Everything happens for a reason,' she philosophized. And, sure enough, one of the album's late arrivals, effectively an afterthought, came to be its defining dynamic glory: the crackling, crystalline 'Crazy in Love'.

Co-written with Rich Harrison, who'd worked with Jennifer Lopez, Amerie and Mary J. Blige, as well as on Kelly Rowland's track 'Can't Nobody', 'Crazy in Love' featured a rap from Jay-Z and – crucially – a horn-section sample from The Chi-Lites' 1970 classic 'Are You My Woman (Tell Me So)', penned by that band's resident soul genius Eugene Record. Harrison had the idea for that hook before he met with Beyoncé, but to his consternation had found that people he was playing it to couldn't 'dig it'. He stuck to his guns, believing he'd hit on something special. Even Beyoncé didn't 'get it' on first listen, expressing doubts about its full-on energy and red-hot fanfare. The notion was also considered perhaps a tad retro for modern audiences. Yet she came around, and gave Harrison a couple of hours to flesh it out. This he did – despite, he's recounted, a raging hangover – with added verses and hooks. Beyoncé, who as it happened that day was dressed down and scruffy by her standards, threw in 'I'm looking so crazy right now' and other ear-catching adornments. The hymn to passionate love's irrationalities and romantic obsession was sounding like a winner.

Jay-Z dropped by the studio around 3a.m. and made up his rap in a few minutes. And so was born one of the best and biggest-selling singles in pop's rich history. Released on 18 May 2003 as the lead for the debut album, it was an instant number one in the US and the UK, eventually passing eight million sales globally. It was deemed the greatest song of its decade by VH1 and by *NME*, while *Rolling Stone* placed it in the top three of the 2000s. 'The horns weren't a hook, they were a herald,' announced the latter. 'Pop's new queen had arrived.' It won Grammys for Best R&B Song and Best Rap/Sung Collaboration. It also won Best Song at the MTV Europe Music Awards. E! retrospectively named it Beyoncé's best musical moment, raving 'It's the song that started it all. The definitive best Beyoncé jam is her first, complete with a guest spot by now-husband Jay-Z, a killer hook and a chorus of horns that you have to dance to. Literally have to, Pavlovian-conditioning style.' Even in 2013, *NME* was listing it 'Best Pop Song of the Century'.

In 2011, Beyoncé perhaps overstated Jay-Z's importance to the number's power and pizazz, underselling her own, when she reflected to *Billboard*: "'Crazy

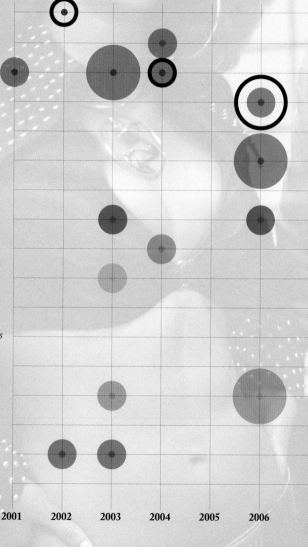

# AND THE AWARD *goes to*...

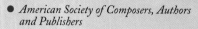

As a winner and nominee across a wide range of genres, including TV, film and the internet, Beyoncé's creativity and charisma proves irrepressible whatever she turns her talents to.

- *American Society of Composers, Authors and Publishers*
- *Black Entertainment Television Awards*
- *Black Reel Awards*
- *Broadcast Film Critics Ass. Awards*
- *Cannes Lions Intern. Festival of Creativity*
- *Golden Globe Awards*
- *Golden Raspberry Awards*
- *MTV Movie Awards*
- *National Association for the Advancement of Colored People Image Awards*
- *Nickelodeon Kids' Choice Awards*
- *Nouvelle Radio des Jeunes Awards*
- *Online Film & Television Association Awards*
- *Primetime Emmy Awards*
- *Satellite Awards*
- *Screen Actors Guild Awards*
- *Teen Choice Awards*
- *Webby Awards*

2001    2002    2003    2004    2005    2006

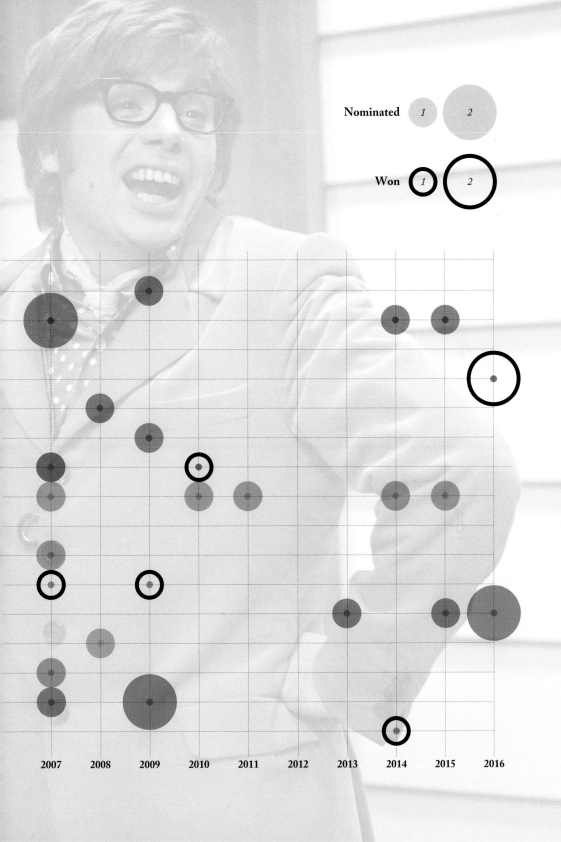

Nominated *1* *2*

Won *1* *2*

2007 2008 2009 2010 2011 2012 2013 2014 2015 2016

in Love" was another one of those classic moments in pop culture that none of us expected. I asked Jay to get on the song the night before I had to turn my album in – thank God he did. It still never gets old, no matter how many times I sing it.' *The Times*, however, pointed out that although Jay-Z's rap was 'decent', 'Beyoncé and the beats save the day'. Jake Nava's video also helped the song to go forth and multiply. Filmed in downtown LA, it saw Beyoncé as a 'crazy-in-love girl', dancing in a white vest and blue shorts that leave just the right amount, though little more, to the imagination. There are fast-paced choreography, costume changes and scenes of Beyoncé entwined with Jay-Z. On the back of the video, Beyoncé was described by the *Philadelphia Enquirer* as having a 'famously photogenic goddess frame'. There were many more lust-fuelled comments, but what was happening here was a performer laying claim to a fiercer, more dangerous and more self-driven identity than she'd had space for within the softer, safer boundaries of Destiny's Child. The much-discussed video, like the song, did its job: Beyoncé wasn't now just a star, she was a pop icon.

'Crazy in Love' was an insane, impossible-to-ignore impact-bomb, all the more so when it served as the soundtrack for one of twenty-one-year-old Beyoncé's Pepsi ads. Prior to the album's release she'd supplanted Britney Spears as what marketing gurus called 'the voice of the Pepsi generation'. As a result, she would make two TV commercials, as well as radio and internet ads, and Pepsi sponsored her next tour.

In fact, so huge was 'Crazy in Love' that the album's subsequent singles had to battle to cling on in its wake, but by any normal standards they performed extremely well. 'Baby Boy', a Storch co-production with Jamaican reggae star Sean Paul guesting, boldly included Indian, Eastern and dancehall influences. It charted while 'Crazy in Love' was still number one, taking the top spot itself eight weeks on. 'Me, Myself and I', another Storch-Knowles production, was something of an Eighties throwback about misbehaving boyfriends. Beyoncé's vocals won acclaim, and the single kept the album flying. Released in March 2004, the fourth single, 'Naughty Girl', was a sex-charged R&B/disco cut that dropped in interpolations from Donna Summer's steamy Seventies slinker 'Love to Love You Baby', the track that had made legendary producer Giorgio Moroder's name. (He was credited among the writers.) In the video – again directed by Jake Nava – Beyoncé paid tribute to Hollywood dance deities Cyd Charisse and Fred Astaire,

though moving more salaciously than they ever did opposite the equally nimble Usher. It won Best Female Video at the MTV Video Music Awards that year.

Had Beyoncé successfully transitioned from girl band cutie to globe-dominating solo pop icon? Hell, yes. *Dangerously in Love* had a few weaker elements – an overly saccharine track called 'Daddy' was arguably best forgotten – but its strong points blew away all resistance. And it was clear that Beyoncé had ambitions for the album beyond anything she'd achieved to date. 'I wanted to have an album that everyone could relate to, and would listen to as long as I'm alive … and even after,' she told MTV. 'Love is something that never goes out of style. It's something everybody experiences, and even if people are not in love, they usually WANT to feel it …'

Bizarrely, with hindsight, Columbia had not been overly thrilled by the album before its release, claiming it lacked hit singles. So much for their powers of prediction. Still Beyoncé's biggest album to date, it made her a matchlessly marketable figure, a sex symbol and a magnet for lucrative marketing deals, of which the Pepsi tie-in was just one. Could Destiny's Child survive her newfound solo superpowers? And could they survive being outgrown by Beyoncé's relationship with Jay-Z? As Beyoncé sang the national anthem at Super Bowl XXXVIII, on 1 February 2004, she seemed poised to embrace her own hyper-star status. That she was singing at the Reliant Stadium in Houston, her hometown, just made it all the more resonant. Had she ever dared to dream, growing up there as a child, that she'd be singing 'The Star-Spangled Banner' to such a vast audience? Almost certainly, yes.

**RIGHT:** Beyoncé holds the award for Best Female Video for 'Crazy in Love' at the MTV Music Awards in 2003.

# SIX DEGREES OF *Queen Bey*

It's no surprise that music moguls the world over share their talent pool and collaborate. Many have teamed up with Queen Bey to make sweet music over the years, but that's not where their connections stop.

## BEYONCÉ COLLABORATIONS     → FEATURING ARTIST

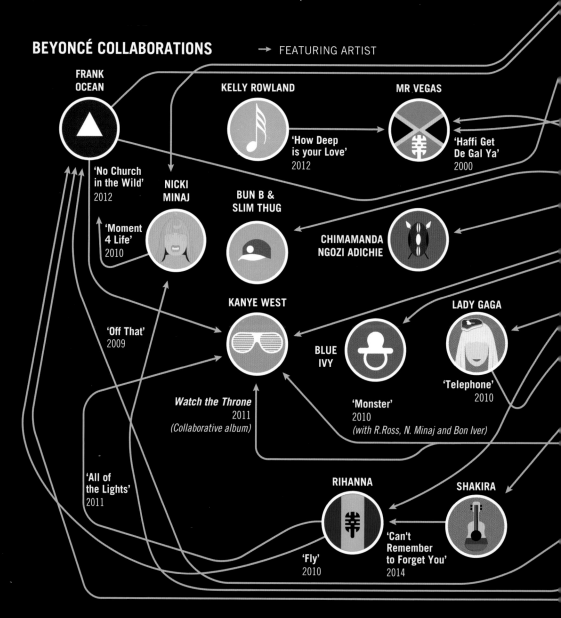

**FRANK OCEAN**

**KELLY ROWLAND**

'How Deep is your Love' 2012

**MR VEGAS**

'Haffi Get De Gal Ya' 2000

'No Church in the Wild' 2012

**NICKI MINAJ**

'Moment 4 Life' 2010

**BUN B & SLIM THUG**

**CHIMAMANDA NGOZI ADICHIE**

'Off That' 2009

**KANYE WEST**

**BLUE IVY**

**LADY GAGA**

'Telephone' 2010

*Watch the Throne* 2011 *(Collaborative album)*

'Monster' 2010 *(with R.Ross, N. Minaj and Bon Iver)*

'All of the Lights' 2011

**RIHANNA**

**SHAKIRA**

'Can't Remember to Forget You' 2014

'Fly' 2010

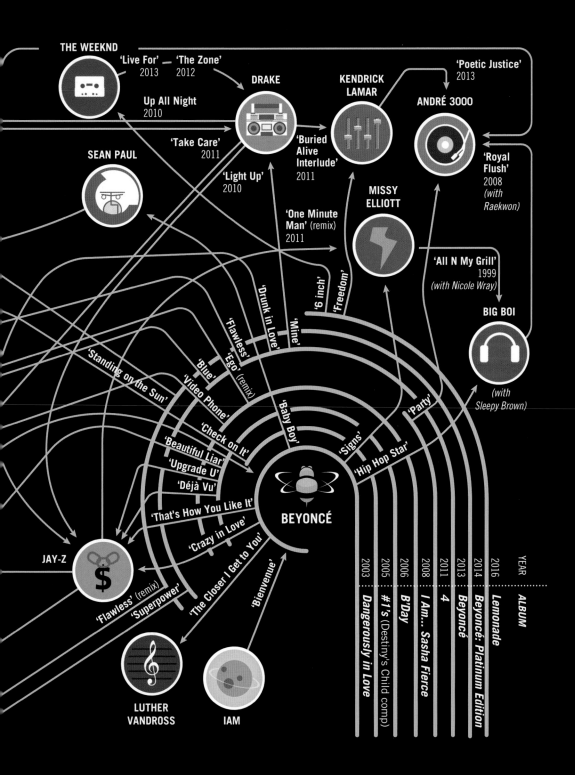

THE WEEKND

'Live For' — 'The Zone'
2013        2012

DRAKE

KENDRICK
LAMAR

'Poetic Justice'
2013

ANDRÉ 3000

Up All Night
2010

SEAN PAUL

'Take Care'
2011

'Buried
Alive
Interlude'
2011

'Royal
Flush'
2008
(with
Raekwon)

'Light Up'
2010

MISSY
ELLIOTT

'One Minute
Man' (remix)
2011

'All N My Grill'
1999
(with Nicole Wray)

BIG BOI

(with
Sleepy Brown)

'6 inch'
'Freedom'
'Mine'

'Drunk in Love'

'Flawless'

'Ego' (remix)

'Blue'

'Video Phone'

'Standing on the Sun'

'Check on It'

'Baby Boy'

'Signs'

'Hip Hop Star'

'Party'

'Beautiful Liar'

'Upgrade U'

'Déjà Vu'

BEYONCÉ

'That's How You Like It'

'Crazy in Love'

JAY-Z

'Flawless' (remix)

'Superpower'

'The Closer I Get to You'

'Bienvenue'

LUTHER
VANDROSS

IAM

| YEAR | ALBUM |
|------|-------|
| 2003 | *Dangerously in Love* |
| 2005 | *#1's* (Destiny's Child comp) |
| 2006 | *B'Day* |
| 2008 | *I Am... Sasha Fierce* |
| 2011 | *4* |
| 2013 | *Beyoncé* |
| 2014 | *Beyoncé: Platinum Edition* |
| 2016 | *Lemonade* |

5

# DESTINY FULFILLED

As recently as July 2016, Britain's Channel 5 TV announced a list of the most powerful celebrity couples in the world. The rankings were based on combined media impact, reputed wealth and political influence. It was a non-scientific, controversial, click-baiting list, signalled by the fact that at a lowly number ten were Barack and Michelle Obama. Nevertheless, it made fascinating reading. Moving up the list, from numbers nine to two, it went: Brad Pitt and Angelina Jolie, Rupert Murdoch and Jerry Hall, Kanye West and Kim Kardashian, Elton John and David Furnish, David and Victoria Beckham, Hillary and Bill Clinton, Her Majesty the Queen and Prince Philip, and Bill and Melinda Gates. Top of the couples? You've guessed it – Beyoncé and Jay-Z.

Now while such lists are by nature provocative and in part absurd, many more reputable lists such as *Forbes*, *Business Insider* and *Time* magazine have also scored Beyoncé and Jay-Z highly, both singly and together. So perhaps the most interesting facet of this chart was that Beyoncé and Jay-Z's placing at the pinnacle didn't seem entirely bonkers. They've never been in charge of the nuclear codes, but they're certainly as famous and globally recognizable as anyone else alive in the twenty-first century. And they're clearly no flash in the pan: they've sustained this level of fame, as a pair, for almost a decade and a half, and it seems unlikely to subside.

They first met in October 2001, at the Concert for New York City, which took place at Madison Square Garden shortly after the 9/11 attacks. The audience was made up of heroic NYPD and FDNY officers and other rescue workers. Destiny's Child appeared, as did a host of A-list names including David Bowie, Paul McCartney, The Who, Bon Jovi, Backstreet Boys, Eric Clapton, Mick Jagger, Elton John, Billy Joel and one Jay-Z. Beyoncé was twenty; Jay-Z twelve years her senior.

Jay-Z was already a multi-millionaire superstar when the couple met. Shawn Corey Carter – his real name – was arguably the biggest rapper in the business,

Beyoncé $54 m

Jay-Z $53.3 m

$54.5 million

$107.3 million

Alicia Keys $44 m

Swizz Beatz $10.5 m

Tom Brady $44 m

Gisele Bündchen $30.5 m

$74.5 million

Kim Kardashian $51 m

$68.5 million

Kanye West $17.5 m

# POWER *couple*

When you think of mega power couples, Queen Bey and her king, Jay-Z reign over us all. But hot on their heels are some other highly paid husband and wife teams, who are taking their love straight to the bank. Here is an overview of their 2016 earnings.

and had his own record label and clothing line. He was on his way to being one of the most significant music executives in the industry. Beyoncé was appropriately impressed. 'I admire his ability to inspire others,' she told *Harper's Bazaar* many years later. 'To me, Jay represents the American dream. I respect him so much: he is a great man and a great artist.'

By 2001, Jay-Z albums such as *Reasonable Doubt*, *In My Lifetime Vol. 1*, *Vol. 2... Hard Knock Life*, *The Dynasty: Roc La Familia* and *The Blueprint* had been received as landmarks in the hip-hop genre. If nothing else, then, even before they met he and Beyoncé clearly shared an appetite and talent for success. But Jay-Z's road to the top had been slightly bumpier – hangovers from a childhood that was peppered with violence. He's redeemed himself since as an artist and

## 'I ADMIRE HIS ABILITY TO INSPIRE OTHERS.'

philanthropist, and his net worth in 2016 was estimated at around $550 million. He's sold more than one hundred million records, won twenty-one Grammys and goes from strength to strength as an entrepreneur.

Where Beyoncé had been raised in middle-class suburbia, by contrast Carter grew up in the rather more dangerous Marcy Projects neighbourhood in Brooklyn. He witnessed his first shooting at the age of nine, and was shot at himself in his teens. He told the BBC later: 'We had great days and played outside ... a normal childhood. But some days, when it got bad, people were even shooting at twelve noon on Sundays.' The devil behind the conflict was crack, one of the most addictive street drugs. 'It was a plague,' he reflected. 'It was just everywhere, everywhere you looked. You could smell it in the hallways.'

These early traumas were to colour his lyrics for years to come. Conversely, as a child, his love of music gave him a glimmer of hope of escape. His childhood favourite was Michael Jackson, then he grew into hip-hop. His parents, he recalled, had a massive record collection. 'Everyone came to our house to listen to music and have fun.' It seems his knack for wordplay was innate, and he quickly developed a reputation as the best rapper on the block. He was eager, and driven, too. Instead of daydreaming and waiting for a record deal to drop into his lap, he gave an early sign of his business smarts by selling his CDs from

**LEFT:** Beyoncé and Jay-Z perform at the 2003 MTV Video Music Awards, New York.

the boot of his car. Along with friends Damon Dash and Kareem 'Biggs' Burke, he started the label Roc-A-Fella Records, an independent outlet run through Priority Records, in 1995, aged twenty-five. A distribution deal with Priority saw his debut, *Reasonable Doubt*, make his name. With buzz growing, a link-up with Def Jam ensued for his second album, produced by Sean 'Puff Daddy' Combs, and its raw biographical elements helped to propel it to platinum status. Pretty soon he was winning Grammys and duetting with Mariah Carey. *The Dynasty: Roc La Familia*, released in 2000, saw a more soulful side to his music and enlisted upcoming producers such as The Neptunes and Kanye West, and sold two million copies in the US alone. *The Blueprint*, one of hip-hop's all-time classic albums, was released in the wake of the 9/11 tragedies and perhaps

# FILMOGRAPHY *timeline*

The big screen loves Beyoncé almost as much as the music world and she's fast notching up starring roles in some major movies, further consolidating her all-round iconic status.

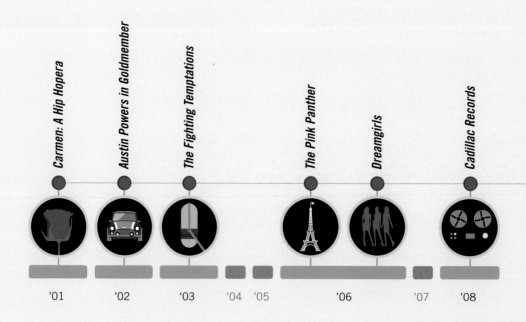

Carmen: A Hip Hopera

Austin Powers in Goldmember

The Fighting Temptations

The Pink Panther

Dreamgirls

Cadillac Records

'01    '02    '03    '04 '05    '06    '07 '08

caught a nerve, going straight in at number one with close to half a million sales in its opening week. Although its media profile was of course overshadowed by real-life events, it went double platinum. Jay-Z claimed to have written all the words in just two days.

So the man Beyoncé met in late 2001 at the Madison Square Garden show was one for whom everything was happening. Though he still carried with him an edgy current, he clearly didn't need to fabricate the loved-up atmosphere or the bad-boy image for the '03 Bonnie & Clyde' video that they were to shoot together the following year.

And yet for a very long time the couple kept their fans guessing, Beyoncé protesting for ages that they were just friends, until that '03 Bonnie & Clyde' video effectively spilled the beans. They were 'friends' with a lot in common. They shared a love of music, of course, and both had a tough work ethic. 'Being broke is a great motivator,' said Carter, referring to his upbringing. And Beyoncé

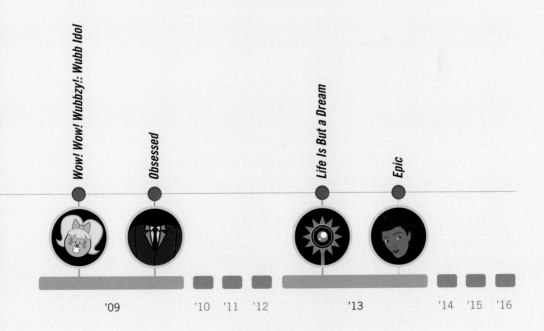

had had the work bug since she was a child.

While the couple were happy to flaunt it on camera, they kept any details of their blossoming relationship private from the press. 'I've learned that it's better if I don't talk about my personal life relationships,' Beyoncé told *Glamour* in 2003. The media were hooked anyway. Their and our fascination with the Bonnie and Clyde union of the golden girl and the bad boy would run and run …

Meanwhile, Beyoncé's career was continuing to smartly diversify. Almost an afterthought in the trail of the comet that was *Dangerously in Love* was the 'upbeat, inspirational' movie *The Fighting Temptations*, which saw a release in late 2003. It was a minor box-office hit, but everyone agreed on one thing: Beyoncé's rendition of 'Fever' was hotter than Georgia asphalt. The comedy-drama was directed by experienced Brit Jonathan Lynn, who'd helmed such oddities as *Nuns on the Run*, *Sgt. Bilko* and the Joe Pesci and Marisa Tomei comedy *My Cousin Vinny*, and saw Cuba Gooding Jr trying to get his Georgia hometown church choir into a gospel competition. Meanwhile he falls back in love with his childhood crush, Beyoncé's Lilly. All ends happily, in large part thanks to a soundtrack featuring a theme song by Beyoncé, Missy Elliott, MC Lyte and Free. Destiny's Child's 'I Know' is also in there, as are tracks by Faith Evans and The O'Jays. Yet it's Beyoncé who dominates the score, duetting on 'Everything I Do' with Bilal, singing 'Time to Come Home' with Angie Stone and Melba Moore, and accompanying Walter Williams Sr on 'He Still Loves Me'. She also uses lessons learned during the church-going years of her youth to perform 'Swing Low, Sweet Chariot', and – on the album but not in the film – sings 'Summertime' with P. Diddy. For his part, Gooding Jr was beaming away on chat shows for a long time afterwards about the joys of kissing Beyoncé. 'Lord, she was wonderful,' he grinned. She spoke of kissing scenes (with anyone, not specifically him) being embarrassing and uncomfortable.

Beyoncé's role was a marked contrast to the flirty fun of her Austin Powers calling card. Yes, it gave her lots of opportunity to sing, but when we meet Lilly

**LEFT:** Beyoncé and her co-star Cuba Gooding Jr at the premiere of *The Fighting Temptations* in 2003.

she's a single mum singing in bars to make ends meet. Beyoncé, promoting the movie, told a TV show: 'The music is incredible. The message is incredible. You want to take your parents to see it, your kids to see it …' Being around the church made her 'feel at home', she told CBS News. 'It's about coming home and finding what's important to you.'

She'd been taking acting lessons, which she said had taught her much about herself. 'I've learned you have to pull from things and think about things that I'd never really thought about. I'm sure it's also going to definitely inspire me to write different songs and different types of music.' The experience possibly enabled her to fully inhabit characters in some of her subsequent songs: she was to go on to 'be' Sasha Fierce, of course, and then shed inhibitions further on her albums of the 2010s.

Elsewhere in the press she spoke of her love of gospel, and, when asked about inspiration, in terms of singers becoming actors, praised Barbra Streisand and Diana Ross, in particular their performances in *Mahogany* and *Lady Sings the Blues*. 'They were singers and were successful and did not have to act for financial or any other reasons, but they did because they wanted to. And they loved it and were talented and gifted. I don't think there's anything wrong with combining music and film.' She then added, 'But I do want to eventually do a movie where I'm not a singer …'

However, she'd be so busy that her next film wouldn't be for three years. In the meantime, the next step was orchestrating a graceful exit from Destiny's

**LEFT:** Beyoncé, Kelly and Michelle dressed in traditional Japanese kimonos on their Destiny Fulfilled... and Lovin' It tour, Tokyo, 2005.

Child. After the success of *Dangerously in Love*, there was no question now that Beyoncé should go solo, but the girls were still great friends and everyone involved wanted to wrap the band up in a healthy spirit. Initially, it seemed, there was some uncertainty about how to proceed. At one point Mathew Knowles announced that his younger daughter, Solange, had joined Destiny's Child, making them a quartet again. But in 2003 Beyoncé declared that wasn't in fact happening, and all concerned were effusive in support of Solange's solo debut album, *Solo Star*.

Beyoncé must have been hard-pressed to stay loyal to all those making demands of her. After her Super Bowl starring role she'd planned to begin on a follow-up to *Dangerously in Love*, but then decided to make her next project a Destiny's Child album, *Destiny Fulfilled*. This fifth and final group album – bar a greatest hits compilation – saw the group's hiatus ended, but also marked the end of their active lifetime as a trio. Already their increasing independence was evident, as Kelly and Michelle

> 'THE MAIN THING IS THAT WE MAINTAIN OUR FRIENDSHIP AND DO IT BECAUSE WE WANT TO – NOT BECAUSE IT'S A GOOD BUSINESS MOVE.'

contributed to writing and producing as much as Beyoncé. (Whether this was a newfound democratic logic, or simply down to her being too busy, is debatable.) Guaranteed class acts in writing and production collaboration such as Rodney Jerkins, Rich Harrison, Rockwilder and Swizz Beatz were brought in, everyone aware that this was the trio's collective swansong.

It does seem as if the three saw this album as a personal passion, and were relatively less concerned with chart placings than with telling heartfelt stories about the way they felt about their lives' trajectories. 'We did this record for ourselves, not to sell a million the first week out,' shrugged Beyoncé calmly. Kelly confided that she was getting older and wanted to end on a high note, giving the fans a great finale. And although solo stardom beckoned, Beyoncé was keen to keep all avenues open. 'Who knows what will happen in three, five, or ten years?' she said. 'The main thing is that we maintain our friendship and do it because we want to – not because it's a good business move.'

While it can be easy to be cynical about such protestations, the girls really were, and are, friends. People asked the girls why they made *Destiny Fulfilled*, and

Beyoncé explained to MTV News:

> We're friends. We enjoy each other. We sound good together. We grew
> up together and hopefully we can set an example for other female
> groups that you can support each other and not be insecure and can
> be happy for one another. And it's OK to do solo projects and to grow
> up and get a life. But it's also OK to come back together. It doesn't
> always have to be what the media tries to make it out to be. Women
> can get along, and be businesswomen, and be smart, and not be catty
> all the time.

This avowal of sisterhood and shrewd showbiz acumen rang true: the young
women hung out and worked together one more time because they liked
each other's company and took creative pleasure in their years of honing their
harmonies.

Some might argue that their commitment to each other was stronger than
the actual album, but it nonetheless performed as well as critics and fans alike had
come to expect. It was pitched as a linear story about a group of women searching
for love – who then find it when they learn to love themselves. Opener 'Lose
My Breath' raced in with military rhythms, sound effects and huge energy, with
Rodney and Fred Jerkins on the controls, and second single 'Soldier' (featuring
T.I. and Lil Wayne) kept up the heat. Later there are Motown and funk influences,
break-up ballads and elements of gospel.

'Lose My Breath' sold half a million in the States, 'Soldier' did too, whilst
'Girl' and 'Cater 2 U' kept their name in the singles chart. The album went to
number one on the Top R&B/Hip-Hop chart, and was certified triple platinum
within two months. A vast worldwide tour followed, named Destiny Fulfilled…
and Lovin' It. It was their last together. In America alone it grossed $70 million,
a figure that surpassed any pop or R&B tour since the 1999 TLC tour on which
Destiny's Child had been the opening act. It ran from Hiroshima in Japan in
April 2005 to Vancouver in Canada in September. They performed band hits
and solo hits, with the balance leaning slightly towards Beyoncé's blockbusters.

In June, onstage in Barcelona, Kelly did a Ziggy Stardust and announced
that this was their last tour as Destiny's Child, though most had already assumed

this would be the case. She declared that after working together since they were nine, and touring since they were fourteen, much discussion and soul-searching had led to the decision that this was the perfect opportunity to leave on a high, united and filled with gratitude. They were to pursue 'personal goals and solo efforts in earnest'. She emphasized that 'no matter what', they'd always love each other as friends and sisters.

Beyoncé concurred. 'It's the end of this chapter in our lives. Our destinies have been fulfilled.' They would work together on the million-selling greatest hits compilation *#1's*, which premiered three new songs and would see the trio reunite to accept a star on the Hollywood Walk of Fame in March 2006, and again for *Love Songs* in 2013. But Destiny's Child was over.

It's hard not to feel overawed by Beyoncé's work ethic during this period. The group's closing chapter was enough to more than fill most artists' plates, or diaries. Yet she was pressing on with her solo profile and amping up the hip (hop) associations, not least through her relationship with Jay-Z.

## 'IT'S THE END OF THIS CHAPTER IN OUR LIVES. OUR DESTINIES HAVE BEEN FULFILLED.'

Back in August 2003 the couple had stolen the show at the MTV Music Awards at New York's Radio City. She'd made quite an entrance. Suspended upside down from the ceiling, she was lowered down while singing 'Baby Boy', then launched into 'Crazy in Love'. It was a triumphant night all round for her, as 'Crazy in Love' collected wins for Best R&B Video, Best Female Video and Best Choreography.

The Dangerously in Love Tour of November 2003 had seen two nights filmed at Wembley Arena in London for a CD/DVD, which was soon released as *Live at Wembley*. It caused even country star Miranda Lambert to comment, 'She's the ultimate diva. The charisma, the confidence …' Critics spoke of the beaming smile on Beyoncé's face being as big as their own, and only the *Guardian's* Dave Simpson struck a rare sour note, complaining that she felt like a cross between 'Liza Minnelli showbiz and thumping R&B'. Yet this was Beyoncé in the process of transitioning from her pop princess role within Destiny's Child to an edgier, more streetwise solo persona. While it may have frustrated a few, her fans were ready for and open to the change, more than happy for the star to shine in a

# BETTER
*to be*
*single!*

Every single that Beyoncé releases is met with adoration by her fans. The graphic below shows her single versus album sales, charting which singles had the greatest success. Singles and albums are only represented here if they have been released for more than a year and sold over one million copies.

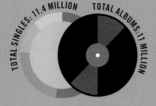

- 'Crazy in Love' **6 MILLION**
- 'Baby Boy' **2.7 MILLION**
- 'Naughty Girl' **1.4 MILLION**
- 'Me, Myself and I' **1.3 MILLION**

TOTAL SINGLES: 11.4 MILLION
TOTAL ALBUMS: 11 MILLION

*DANGEROUSLY IN LOVE*

**2003**

- 'Irreplaceable' **8.5 MILLION**
- 'Déjà Vu' **1.5 MILLION**
- 'Ring the Alarm' **1.4 MILLION**

TOTAL SINGLES: 11.4 MILLION
TOTAL ALBUMS: 8 MILLION

*B'DAY*

**2006**

TOTAL SINGLES: 33.2MILLION

- 'Single Ladies' **10.5 MILLION**
- 'Halo' **9.5 MILLION**
- 'If I Were a Boy' **6.5 MILLION**
- 'Sweet Dreams' **3.2 MILLION**
- 'Diva' **2 MILLION**
- 'Ego' **1.5 MILLION**

TOTAL ALBUMS: 7 MILLION

*I AM... SASHA FIERCE*

**2008**

TOTAL SINGLES: 11 MILLION

TOTAL ALBUM: 3 MILLION

*4*

**2011**

- 'Love on Top' **3.5 MILLION**
- 'Best Thing I Never Had' **3.5 MILLION**
- 'Run the World (Girls)' **3 MILLION**
- 'Countdown' **1 MILLION**

- 'Drunk in Love' **3.3 MILLION**
- 'Partition' **1.3 MILLION**
- 'XO' **1.3 MILLION**
- '***Flawless' **1 MILLION**

TOTAL SINGLES: 6.9 MILLION

TOTAL ALBUM: 3.7 MILLION

*BEYONCÉ*

**2013**

multiplicity of genres on the way to merging them in her own unique fashion.

If Beyoncé's rendition of the national anthem at the Super Bowl had been denied front pages by the perfect media storm of Janet Jackson's infamous 'wardrobe malfunction' with Justin Timberlake, she was determined to boss the 2004 Grammy Awards show. Invited to open alongside another of her idols, Prince, in a medley of his hits, she was so excited that even she – no stranger now to high-pressure shows – got nervous.

'I was terrified, walking into rehearsals, so overwhelmed and nervous and star-struck! We rehearsed every day for an hour for a week. That was Prince's idea, as he knows people are star-struck … it made me really comfortable. So by the time it came to do it, it was second nature.'

She looked so confident when the night came that it won raves as another of her significant star-status-stealing performances. As she and Prince raced through sections of 'Purple Rain', 'Let's Go Crazy', 'Baby I'm a Star' and her own 'Crazy in Love', even in this company it was Beyoncé who seemed to be the essence of swagger. In fact, according to some reports, she worried that she'd hogged the microphone, not giving the great man himself enough limelight. Her Sasha Fierce alter ego, still to be introduced to her legion of fans, was already in the house, owning it. Beyoncé won five Grammys that night, performed again (a slightly more relaxed 'Dangerously in Love 2'), and then thanked her parents, her producers and Kelly and Michelle in her acceptance speech.

When you've nudged Prince out of the spotlight, you know you're fierce, and Beyoncé was firing up new impulses and synapses in her onstage character. It was her parade now, and nobody was going to rain on it.

**LEFT:** Beyoncé and Prince perform together at the 46th Annual Grammy Awards in LA, 2004.

6

# DREAM GIRL

**B**eyoncé was attracting almost as much heat and light as she was emitting. Whilst 2005 saw her wrapping up her time with Destiny's Child, 2006 was another relentless year for her solo career. With the romance with Jay-Z continuing – as privately as possible – Beyoncé found time to release two major Hollywood movies and the much anticipated follow-up album to her debut dynamo.

First was Shawn Levy's reboot of *The Pink Panther*, an attempt to kick-start the famous franchise into a new era, with Steve Martin taking on the role of Inspector Clouseau. Supporting cast in the new version included Kevin Kline, Emily Mortimer and Jean Reno. Beyoncé played a famous but mysterious pop star, Xania, who charms Clouseau. Not quite the stretch she'd been hankering for, perhaps, though she performed two songs, 'A Woman Like Me' and the secondary theme song (of course, Henry Mancini's 'The Pink Panther Theme' had to take priority), the irresistibly catchy 'Check on It'.

Beyoncé felt that 'A Woman Like Me' had 'the strength of a Tina Turner song but the drama of a Bond tune … it definitely fits the character'. But it is the second tune, 'Check on It', that ranks as one of the great, but comparatively underrated, cuts in the Beyoncé pop canon. It still went to number one in the US for five weeks, her third gold solo chart-topper. Not originally intended as a single, it was picked up by radio stations and then boosted by a Hype Williams' video that inserted a remix of 'The Pink Panther Theme'. It was sexy and it was popular.

## 'IT WAS MY FIRST ACTING GIG AND I HOPE NOBODY EVER FINDS IT.'

What was less commonly documented was that Beyoncé had worked with the film's director, Shawn Levy, long before, on a Disney sitcom pilot called *The Famous Jett Jackson*. 'It was my first acting gig and I hope nobody ever finds it,' she confided to IGN.com. 'He [Levy] remembered me and called and told me about Xania, that she was an international superstar singer.' Then Beyoncé revealed a charmingly self-deprecating sense of humour. 'At first I thought I didn't want to play another part like that,' she said drily, 'because I don't have time to do the research.' Once she learned Steve Martin was in it, though, she had to do it. She studied him closely on set, admiring his professionalism and seriousness, observing that 'in between his takes, he goes from being this wacky, unbelievable character to becoming Steve Martin and working with the director, changing things, writing … As a songwriter and performer I respect that, and hopefully one day I'll do that.' With hindsight, it seems that in praising Martin's ability to transition she was probably hinting at the Beyoncé-Knowles-Sasha-Fierce switch,

**ABOVE:** Beyoncé on the set of *The Pink Panther* in 2009.

which she'd soon open up more about. As with Sasha Fierce later, Beyoncé emphasized that she wasn't really like Xania: 'I'm like that onstage, but I'm not like that in real life. It's a character, it's acting.'

Before her next acting role, which saw her receive a Golden Globe nomination, there was the important matter of the second solo album to attend to. She'd originally hoped to have it out in 2004, to capitalize on the phenomenon of *Dangerously in Love*, but the Destiny's Child reunion and filming commitments

# HIT ALBUM: *B'day*

Released on the same day as Bey's 25th birthday, and with many of the lyrics heavily inspired by her role in the film *Dreamgirls*, her second studio album *B'Day* debuted at number one in the US Billboard 200 Chart and was an international success story.

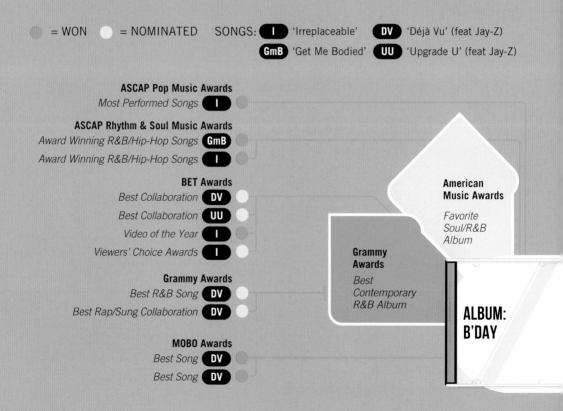

● = WON    ○ = NOMINATED    SONGS:  **I** 'Irreplaceable'   **DV** 'Déjà Vu' (feat Jay-Z)
**GmB** 'Get Me Bodied'   **UU** 'Upgrade U' (feat Jay-Z)

**ASCAP Pop Music Awards**
*Most Performed Songs* **I**

**ASCAP Rhythm & Soul Music Awards**
*Award Winning R&B/Hip-Hop Songs* **GmB**
*Award Winning R&B/Hip-Hop Songs* **I**

**BET Awards**
*Best Collaboration* **DV**
*Best Collaboration* **UU**
*Video of the Year* **I**
*Viewers' Choice Awards* **I**

**Grammy Awards**
*Best R&B Song* **DV**
*Best Rap/Sung Collaboration* **DV**

**MOBO Awards**
*Best Song* **DV**
*Best Song* **DV**

**American Music Awards**
*Favorite Soul/R&B Album*

**Grammy Awards**
Best Contemporary R&B Album

**ALBUM: B'DAY**

had necessitated a delay. It emerged, at last, on 4 September 2006 – Beyoncé's twenty-fifth birthday. Hence the title, *B'Day*, playing also on her pet name, 'B'.

Her profile had, if anything, grown in the gap since her solo debut, and *B'Day* rocketed into the Billboard chart at number one, selling well over half a million in its first week alone. Less expectedly, it was 'Irreplaceable' – the third US single from the album, but only the second release everywhere else – that really took off, becoming the US bestseller of 2007. The usual who's who of contemporary

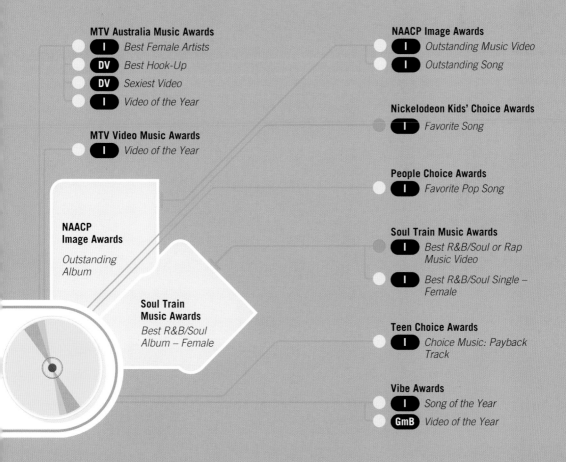

**MTV Australia Music Awards**
- **I**   *Best Female Artists*
- **DV**   *Best Hook-Up*
- **DV**   *Sexiest Video*
- **I**   *Video of the Year*

**MTV Video Music Awards**
- **I**   *Video of the Year*

**NAACP Image Awards**
*Outstanding Album*

**Soul Train Music Awards**
*Best R&B/Soul Album – Female*

**NAACP Image Awards**
- **I**   *Outstanding Music Video*
- **I**   *Outstanding Song*

**Nickelodeon Kids' Choice Awards**
- **I**   *Favorite Song*

**People Choice Awards**
- **I**   *Favorite Pop Song*

**Soul Train Music Awards**
- **I**   *Best R&B/Soul or Rap Music Video*
- **I**   *Best R&B/Soul Single – Female*

**Teen Choice Awards**
- **I**   *Choice Music: Payback Track*

**Vibe Awards**
- **I**   *Song of the Year*
- **GmB**   *Video of the Year*

writer-producers were engaged, including The Neptunes, Rodney Jerkins, Rich Harrison and Swizz Beatz, with Beyoncé co-writing and co-producing. Given her hectic schedule – the shoot for her next film, *Dreamgirls*, having just finished – the bulk of it was recorded over an industrious three weeks.

All the studios at Sony's New York building were locked down and tracks were created simultaneously, with Beyoncé dashing from studio to studio, checking in on and working with the diverse producers. Makeba Riddick, who co-wrote several tracks as part of this ideas hub, stated that they all 'worked together every day, fourteen hours a day' or more. She told MTV, 'I see the reason why she is the biggest star of our generation. Her work ethic is unlike anything I've ever seen.' She recalled that they'd graft from 11a.m. to 4a.m., but each morning after a late night Beyoncé would be back there before anyone else. The album revealed a harder edge in many places, often offering an undiluted, choppy take on Seventies funk grooves and piling layer upon layer of vocals and punchy production. Beyoncé sounded re-energized at times, laying more and more vocal lines over her already multiple charged-up voices until it was like a team of Beyoncés were preaching and testifying.

> **'I SEE THE REASON WHY SHE IS THE BIGGEST STAR OF OUR GENERATION. HER WORK ETHIC IS UNLIKE ANYTHING I'VE EVER SEEN.'**
>
> **MAKEBA RIDDICK**

It went on to win the 2007 Grammy for Best Contemporary R&B Album and score as triple platinum. Seven months on, an anthology of thirteen videos (*B'Day Anthology Video Album*) was released in tandem with the deluxe edition, including her 'Beautiful Liar' collaboration with Shakira, exploring an audio-visual interface that she'd revisit later in her career.

Perhaps the only miscalculation, uncharacteristically, was the choice of the first two singles. 'Déjà Vu', produced by Jerkins and Beyoncé, featuring Jay-Z for a cameo, was intended as a summer anthem, but didn't quite emulate the magic of 'Crazy in Love'. It peaked at number four Stateside.

'Ring the Alarm', at the eleventh hour, usurped 'Green Light' with a US-only release. Its honking, in-your-face sirens gave it a startling, aggressive feel.

**LEFT:** Beyoncé performing at the Honda Center in California as part of The Beyoncé Experience tour in 2007.

# THE ART OF *giving*

Beyoncé has supported, or currently supports these thirty-one charities. She co-founded two charities: the Survivor Foundation, with Kelly Rowland, originally for victims of 2005's Hurricane Katrina, but which went on to support victims of other disasters, and Chime for Change, which promotes education, healthcare and justice for women and girls around the world.

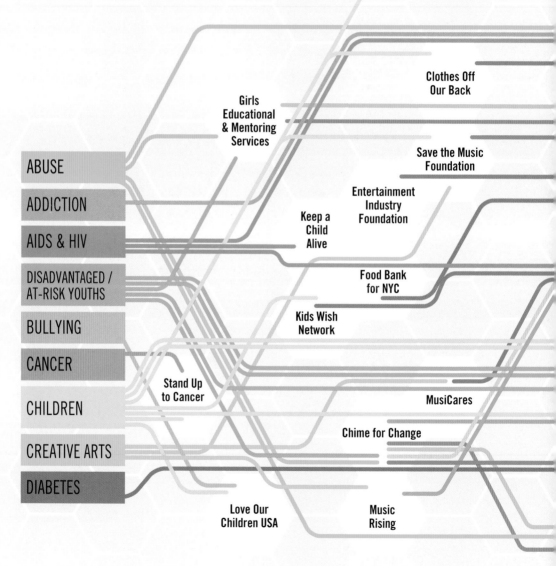

Clothes Off
Our Back

Girls
Educational
& Mentoring
Services

Save the Music
Foundation

ABUSE

ADDICTION

Entertainment
Industry
Foundation

Keep a
Child
Alive

AIDS & HIV

DISADVANTAGED /
AT-RISK YOUTHS

Food Bank
for NYC

Kids Wish
Network

BULLYING

CANCER

Stand Up
to Cancer

MusiCares

CHILDREN

Chime for Change

CREATIVE ARTS

DIABETES

Love Our
Children USA

Music
Rising

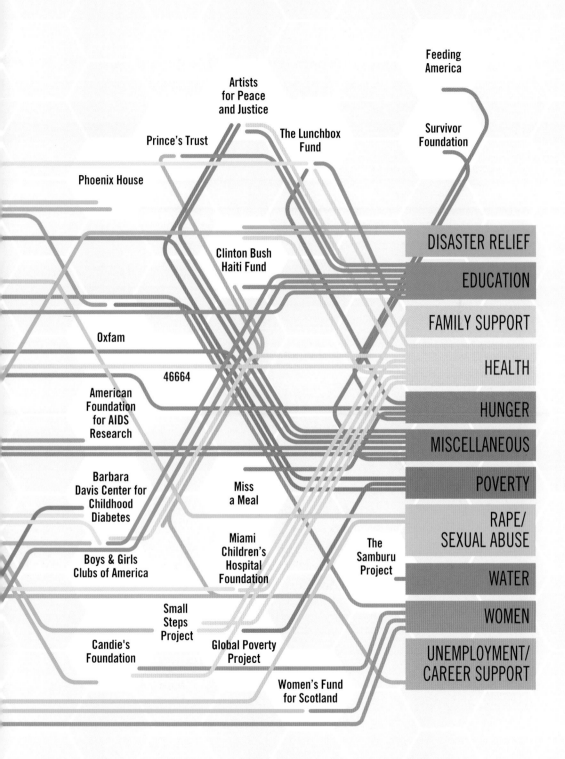

Feeding
America

Survivor
Foundation

Artists
for Peace
and Justice

Prince's Trust

The Lunchbox
Fund

Phoenix House

DISASTER RELIEF

Clinton Bush
Haiti Fund

EDUCATION

FAMILY SUPPORT

Oxfam

HEALTH

46664

HUNGER

American
Foundation
for AIDS
Research

MISCELLANEOUS

Barbara
Davis Center for
Childhood
Diabetes

Miss
a Meal

POVERTY

RAPE/
SEXUAL ABUSE

The
Samburu
Project

Miami
Children's
Hospital
Foundation

Boys & Girls
Clubs of America

WATER

Small
Steps
Project

WOMEN

Candie's
Foundation

Global Poverty
Project

UNEMPLOYMENT/
CAREER SUPPORT

Women's Fund
for Scotland

Rumours spread that it was Beyoncé's warning shot at Rihanna about getting close to Jay-Z: she denied this. Nonetheless, the alleged 'love triangle' swiftly became a silly staple of unscrupulous tabloids always hungry for easy gossip. Some praised the track's bold edge, others bemoaned its jaggedness. An increasingly fearless Beyoncé posed in a swimsuit with baby alligators on the single's cover art.

Despite the respective merits of individual tracks, *B'Day* was not quite able to effortlessly emulate the untroubled rise of Beyoncé's debut solo album. Mathew Knowles may not have helped when he issued a statement claiming there was 'a consistent plan by some to create chaos' around Beyoncé's album, including, he said, 'a rumour regarding conflict between Beyoncé and Rihanna … What will be next? Beyoncé's cut off all her hair? Dyed it green? Maybe she's singing the songs in reverse with some hidden subliminal message?' Clearly, some in Beyoncé's camp were frustrated by the media looking to stir up scandal.

Be that as it may, the third single, 'Irreplaceable', chiefly written by Ne-Yo and produced by Stargate, with co-writing and co-production credits to Beyoncé, set everything back on course. It was a mid-tempo, more conventionally produced song with a hook – 'to the left, to the left' – that made everything all right. Soul Train deemed it the best R&B/Soul Single of 2007 and, in the burgeoning digital age, it became the second Beyoncé single to reach two hundred million 'audience impressions', something only Mariah Carey had previously managed. Needless to say, its themes of infidelity didn't go unnoticed, and some likened Beyoncé to Aretha Franklin or Whitney Houston in her championing of female empowerment within romantic relationships.

On no less a platform than *Larry King Live* on CNN – an indication of how highly Beyoncé ranked now – she said the song was 'honest' and explained that it suggested that 'basically we can't forget our power and our worth. And sometimes you're so in love that you forget that. Sometimes you feel that you're not being appreciated. And sometimes "they" forget that they can be replaced.'

Meanwhile, Beyoncé's biggest and best (in most eyes) film role, *Dreamgirls*, echoed another famed relationship: that between Motown boss Berry Gordy

Jr and his favoured star Diana Ross. Many saw further parallels in the film's narrative with Jay-Z and Beyoncé, though the comparison seems a bit too trite to be credible. In any case, the film itself was a spectacular success, with both the paying public and critics. After sneak previews, *Dreamgirls* was released nationwide on Christmas Day 2006, and was a lovingly wrapped gift for Beyoncé fans. It gave her the acting credibility she'd craved, and played strongly on themes she'd already embraced in her music. And *Dreamgirls* was different from the screen work she'd done before, despite the fact that she was again playing a singer.

**ABOVE:** Bill Condon, Jamie Foxx, Beyoncé, Danny Glover and Jennifer Hudson at the *Dreamgirls* premiere in Paris, 2007.

Both a musical and a high-pitched drama, *Dreamgirls* was adapted from the 1981 stage musical by Henry Krieger and Tom Eyen, which had won six Tony Awards. It had long been mooted as a movie, with Whitney Houston and Lauryn Hill proposed for starring roles at various times. This Bill Condon-directed realization moved the primary action from Chicago to Detroit, but kept the all-important songs. The most expensive film to feature an all African-American lead cast ever made, it saw Jamie Foxx, the debuting Jennifer Hudson, Eddie Murphy, Danny Glover and Anika Noni Rose star alongside Beyoncé. Its 'fictional' tale drew much inspiration from the Motown story, focusing on the rise and ructions of a thinly veiled Supremes (named The Dreams in the film) and their rapport with

their record company head. For all its tempestuous scenes of conflict, it joyously celebrated the ascent of Soul and R&B music through the Sixties and Seventies.

For a hit Broadway musical, *Dreamgirls* was unusually hard-hitting. Motown had been frequently, and quite rightly garlanded, but few had acknowledged its behind-the-scenes dark side. As the story goes here, The Dreams' most talented singer, Effie White (Hudson), is ultimately relegated and rejected by the label head for the more photogenic, if less vocally gifted, Deena Jones (Knowles). Those who'd read up on Florence Ballard and Diana Ross could squint and drum up apparent parallels. Other characters underline the links. Jamie Foxx's Curtis Taylor Jr, a slick, ruthless businessman who ditches Effie for Deena, is comparable to Gordy Jr, and Eddie Murphy's Jimmy 'Thunder' Early is possibly an amalgamation of James Brown, Marvin Gaye and Jackie Wilson. Anika Noni Rose's Lorrel Robinson is perhaps a refracted-through-fiction Mary Wilson, who becomes Early's mistress, whilst other characters bear shades of Cindy Birdsong and Smokey Robinson. It was perhaps inevitable that some viewers would see further parallels between the story of The Dreams and Beyoncé moving on from a group to go solo and pairing up with a powerful player in the music business. Particularly as Beyoncé herself had indicated that Mathew Knowles had modelled aspects of his approach to artist development on that of the Motown founder, noting 'I'm sure he got it out of reading Berry.'

**LEFT:** Jennifer Hudson, Anika Noni Rose and Beyoncé perform 'Patience' from the film *Dreamgirls* at the annual Academy Awards in California, 2007.

The movie was such a major project that even Beyoncé had to lobby and audition. Once Jamie Foxx heard that she and Eddie Murphy were on board, he dropped his salary demands, so delighted and convinced was he by the gathering of star power. Jennifer Hudson, twenty one years old at the time, for many, steals the movie, not least with the showstopper 'And I Am Telling You I'm Not Going'. Rehearsals were extensive for music, choreography and the building of credible relationship dynamics, and reports circulated of Beyoncé losing weight to depict her character's ageing. She lived on a diet of water, lemons, maple syrup and cayenne pepper: and I am telling you, twenty pounds were going. Her own – or Deena's – defining musical highlight was 'Listen', which doubled as the first single from the chart-topping soundtrack album.

*Dreamgirls* was pushed hard for awards by DreamWorks and Paramount. *Variety* had raved about its 'tremendously exciting musical sequences' and pointed out that 'after *Rent, The Phantom of the Opera* and *The Producers* botched the transfer from stage to screen, *Dreamgirls* gets it right'. Hudson was drowned in plaudits, with the influential Oprah Winfrey referring to her performance as 'transcendental' and a 'religious experience'. Eight Oscar nominations rained down, though not, controversially, for Best Picture or Best Director. Both Jennifer Hudson and Eddie Murphy were nominated as actors, and Hudson won. Beyoncé, meanwhile, gained a Best Performance by an Actress in a Motion Picture (Comedy or Musical) nomination at the Golden Globes, where the film won Best Motion Picture (Comedy or Musical). Beyoncé seemed happy and willing to step back and play the supporting (and supportive) role when it came to these awards ceremonies: for her it was about the film being appreciated as a whole. She celebrated Hudson's breakthrough, recognizing in her another star who'd climbed up through hard work and genuine talent.

While Diana Ross, who was said to have felt the stage version had appropriated and twisted her life story, simply said she hadn't seen the film, fellow former Supreme Mary Wilson said it made her cry and that it was closer to what really happened back then than anyone realized. Beyoncé met Ross, having studied her work, and no problems ensued. Other interested parties such as Smokey Robinson claimed to be offended at the portrayal of Gordy Jr as engaging in

**RIGHT:** Beyoncé and her mother, Tina Knowles, at the launch of House of Deréon at Selfridges in London, 2011.

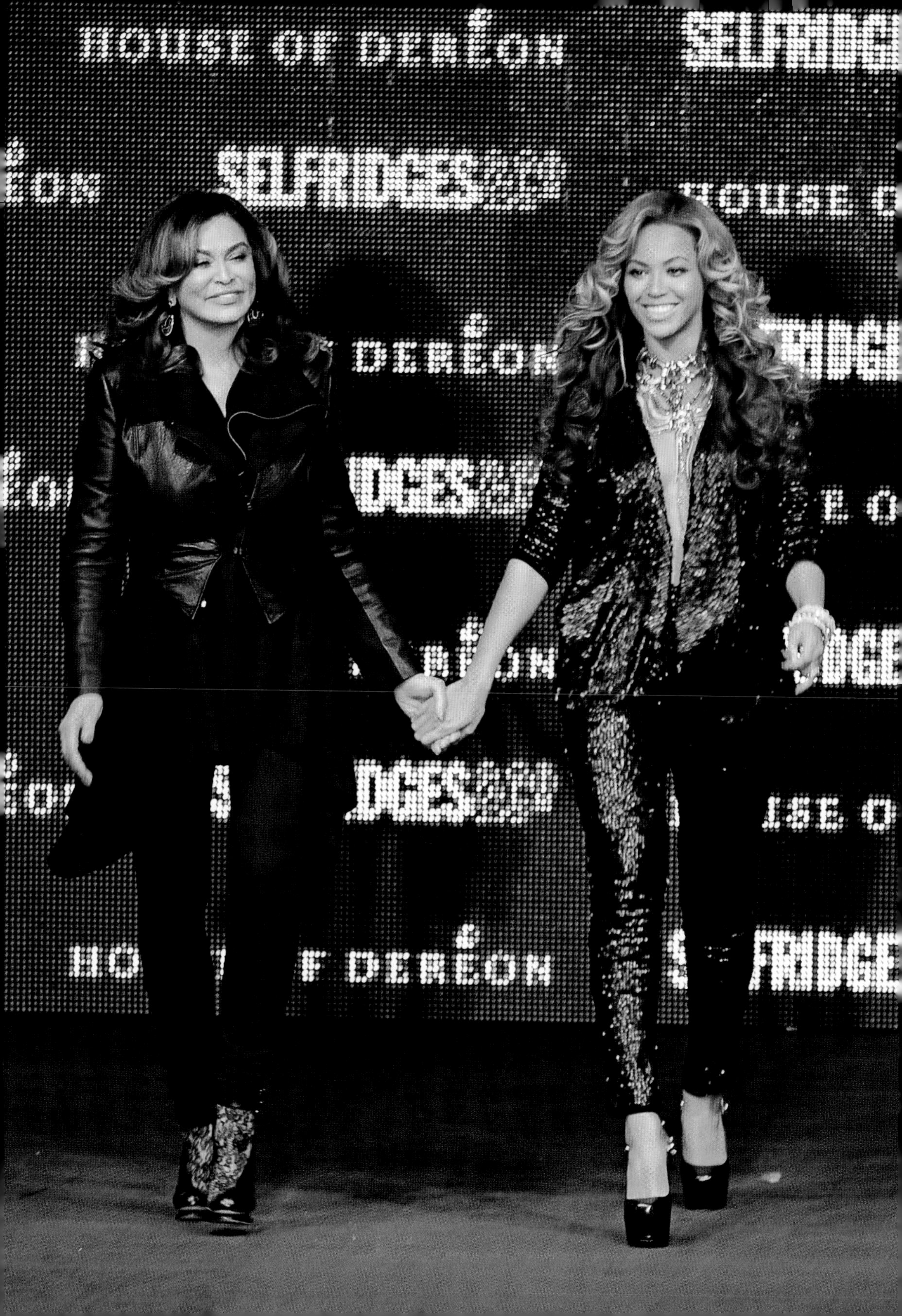
HOUSE OF DEREON
SELFRIDGES

illegal and immoral activities. Belatedly, DreamWorks and Paramount issued an apology to Gordy Jr, who accepted without too much fuss. It's feasible that if anyone had enough experience to suss that all this publicity would get people replaying their Motown records, it would be him.

It was, all in all, a successful venture for Beyoncé. If she wasn't the principal star, she was nonetheless a well-received contributor to a lively and talented ensemble. For most of her musical moments, she does a good Diana Ross impersonation, as required, but such considered restraint isn't natural to

CANADA 18

USA 207

BRAZIL 10

## FLYING *solo*

From 2002 to 2016 Beyoncé slayed the world with her solo tours. This map shows the ten countries where she gave the most concerts within that time period, with her own place of birth coming top, with 207 concerts, and the Netherlands sitting in tenth place.

her. She gets to let rip in something closer to her own peripatetic style on 'Listen' – and fans twigged that it was a hidden track on *B'Day*.

Yet *Dreamgirls* was only one string to her bow. She had somehow found time, too, to launch House of Deréon, a fashion brand she designed with her mother. She had also opened a music venue and media centre in Houston, and graced the cover of *Sports Illustrated* in a yellow bikini. She was the first musician and just the second African-American woman to feature on the cover of the famous annual swimsuit issue, maybe unsurprisingly the most popular issue of

IRELAND 17 UK 79

FRANCE 12    NETHERLANDS 9    JAPAN 11

GERMANY 19

AUSTRALIA 26

the year from a normally sports-focused publication, which has been credited with the rise of various supermodels and the bikini. However, Beyoncé's aura redefined its calibrations, subverting its labels and charging it up with a post-feminist twist. On one level, it was another nudge away from her perceived 'good girl' career beginnings; on another, it was further proof that she was playing with roles, reinventing what was and wasn't perceived as strength in a female celebrity. Meanwhile, House of Deréon – which was distributed through Macy's, Saks, Bloomingdale's et al. – was good business sense. Describing the label, her mother, Tina, said pragmatically, 'It focuses on Beyoncé's fan base', in acknowledgement that the fans' affections were crucial to maintaining the star's appeal. A talented business person listens and learns from the fans, hears what they want, and delivers.

That fan base was also currently welcoming news of Beyoncé's world tour, where she would be backed by a band that gave further signs that she was now constantly thinking of what kind of statement she wished to make. With her father she'd auditioned, and selected, an all-female group, which she named Suga Mama. 'I wanted to get together a group of fierce, talented, hungry, beautiful women and form an all-girl band,' she told MTV. Suga Mama's musical directors were guitarist Bibi McGill and bassist Divinity Roxx.

The global trip, titled The Beyoncé Experience, opened in Tokyo on 10 April 2007, took in almost a hundred venues and grossed a whopping $90 million. Its five legs visited Asia, Australia, North America, Europe and Africa. Ten musicians, ten dancers and three backing vocalists filled the stage, which featured staircases that changed colour and a flotilla of suspended disco balls. Wardrobe changes were frequent and pyrotechnics popped.

At one show in Orlando, Florida, in July, Beyoncé fell spectacularly down the flight of stairs during a particularly heated rendition of 'Ring the Alarm', when her heel caught in the hem of her long coat. A trooper, she got straight back up and carried on. Afterwards she asked the crowd, tongue-in-cheek, if they'd

**RIGHT:** Beyoncé at the *Sports Illustrated* Swimsuit Issue Party in Los Angeles, 2007.

mind not sharing clips of the incident to YouTube, but knew very well that, given the current it-only-happened-if-it's-on-social-media climate, they would. Footage went viral but was removed within two days for copyright infringement. Beyoncé's spokesperson laughed it off, chuckling that the trip was 'a mere spot on an otherwise sensational, flawless show'. The star had, after all, picked the song up instantly without missing a beat. Interviewed about it on CNN later, Beyoncé revealed that she'd hurt her head and chin and been bruised unpleasantly, but that adrenaline kept her going. She added that in fact she'd got a little cross at herself for a highly rare, uncharacteristic error and given a 'crazy' and 'really good' show because of it. All agreed that it was another example of her determination to overcome any obstacles and her sheer class and formidable drive as a live performer. It takes more than a tumble to topple this diva.

> 'SHE CAN SING WITH THE POWER OF A TINA TURNER, DANCE WITH THE MILITARY PRECISION OF A JANET JACKSON, AND DRESS WITH THE OVER-THE-TOP FLAIR OF A CHER.'
>
> *STAR-LEDGER*

There were also serious issues addressed and supported, as she partnered with the charity America's Second Harvest to raise awareness at her North American shows for their campaign to combat hunger in the US. Teaming up with the charity and her minister and friend Pastor Rudy Rasmus, she highlighted the fact that more than thirty-five million Americans regularly struggle to find enough money to eat and the detrimental effect that this can have on children in such families. She promoted food collections held before her concerts and raised cash donations for food banks.

The tour also produced a commercially successful live album and DVD of the 2 September concert at LA's Staples Center, which was released just over two months later – in time for Christmas – as *The Beyoncé Experience Live*.

Fall or no fall, the tour confirmed that Beyoncé's energy and stamina were extraordinary. For such a visually flamboyant show – opening with 'Crazy in Love', closing with 'Irreplaceable' and taking in such set pieces as a lengthy Destiny's Child medley and even a *Dreamgirls* medley – it managed to be equal parts sweaty, funky and sexy. Generally, her gigs blasted thirty songs over around two hours. Critics referenced Busby Berkeley and Prince, and declared it 'the best pop show on the planet'. 'She can sing with the power of a Tina Turner, dance with the military precision of a Janet Jackson, and dress with the over-the-top flair of a Cher,' wrote *Star-Ledger*. 'More than just a concert, it's a state-of the-art arena spectacle: the best that 2007 has offered.' The thing is, Beyoncé was just getting warmed up: in 2008 she was to offer even more. She was about rising, not falling.

7

# SASHA FIERCE GETS MARRIED

'**A**t this point,' said Beyoncé, 'I really know who I am, and I don't feel like I have to put myself in a box. I'm not afraid of taking risks. No one can define me.'

It was early 2008, and Beyoncé now began to defy all expectations of female pop stars. Her wedding was just one indication that she was determined to do things differently. On Friday 4 April 2008, around seven years after they'd first met, Beyoncé and Jay-Z married. They tried to keep it secret, but *People* magazine broke the news that they'd filed their signed wedding licence in Scarsdale, New York, on 1 April – fools for love. The highly confidential ceremony was reportedly attended by Beyoncé's parents, her sister Solange, Kelly Rowland and Michelle Williams. Several personal showbiz celebrity pals made the guest list too. Fellow A-list couple Gwyneth Paltrow and Chris Martin were there, as were Beyoncé's idol Janet Jackson and *Dreamgirls* co-stars Jamie Foxx and Jennifer Hudson (further evidence of the strength of the bonds of friendship that Beyoncé had forged with her co-stars in the film). Also invited were producer-mentors Jermaine Dupri and Wyclef Jean, and fellow-Texan and friend Usher. On the party decks was DJ Cassidy, the young New Yorker whose credentials were untouchably cool.

Amazingly, in the age of instant communication and 24/7 publicity, the couple really did keep things under wraps, refusing to discuss the nuptials for months afterwards. All their guests signed confidentiality agreements and no photos emerged. Even more amazingly, the very next day, Beyoncé reported back to work on the set of her next film, *Cadillac Records*, and Jay-Z went back to duties in his recording studio. The relatively low-key nature of the ceremony and

**RIGHT:** Beyoncé and Jay-Z at the 50th Annual Grammy Awards, LA, 2008.

# RUN THE WORLD *(girls)*

As a feminist icon, Queen Bey is keeping company with some pretty impressive self-made women. Beyoncé was one of the top ten youngest high earners in 2016, with an estimated net worth of $265 million. Not bad for thirty-five!

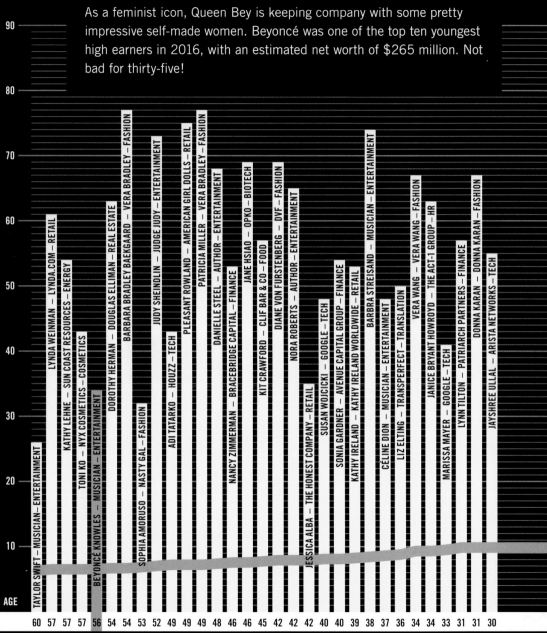

TAYLOR SWIFT — MUSICIAN—ENTERTAINMENT

LYNDA WEINMAN — LYNDA.COM — RETAIL

KATHY LEHNE — SUN COAST RESOURCES — ENERGY

TONI KO — NYX COSMETICS – COSMETICS

BEYONCÉ KNOWLES — MUSICIAN — ENTERTAINMENT

DOROTHY HERMAN — DOUGLAS ELLIMAN — REAL ESTATE

BARBARA BRADLEY BAEKGAARD — VERA BRADLEY — FASHION

SOPHIA AMORUSO — NASTY GAL — FASHION

JUDY SHEINDLIN — JUDGE JUDY — ENTERTAINMENT

ADI TATARKO — HOUZZ — TECH

PLEASANT ROWLAND — AMERICAN GIRL DOLLS — RETAIL

PATRICIA MILLER — VERA BRADLEY — FASHION

DANIELLE STEEL — AUTHOR — ENTERTAINMENT

NANCY ZIMMERMAN — BRACEBRIDGE CAPITAL — FINANCE

JANE HSIAO — OPKO — BIOTECH

KIT CRAWFORD — CLIF BAR & CO — FOOD

DIANE VON FURSTENBERG — DVF — FASHION

NORA ROBERTS — AUTHOR — ENTERTAINMENT

JESSICA ALBA — THE HONEST COMPANY — RETAIL

SUSAN WOJCICKI — GOOGLE — TECH

SONIA GARDNER — AVENUE CAPITAL GROUP — FINANCE

KATHY IRELAND — KATHY IRELAND WORLDWIDE — RETAIL

BARBRA STREISAND — MUSICIAN — ENTERTAINMENT

CÉLINE DION — MUSICIAN — ENTERTAINMENT

LIZ ELTING — TRANSPERFECT — TRANSLATION

VERA WANG — VERA WANG — FASHION

JANICE BRYANT HOWROYD — THE ACT-1 GROUP — HR

MARISSA MAYER — GOOGLE — TECH

LYNN TILTON — PATRIARCH PARTNERS — FINANCE

DONNA KARAN — DONNA KARAN — FASHION

JAYSHREE ULLAL — ARISTA NETWORKS — TECH

AGE

60  57  57  57  56  54  54  53  52  49  49  49  48  46  46  45  42  42  42  40  40  39  38  37  36  34  34  33  31  31  30

**RANKING BY WEALTH**

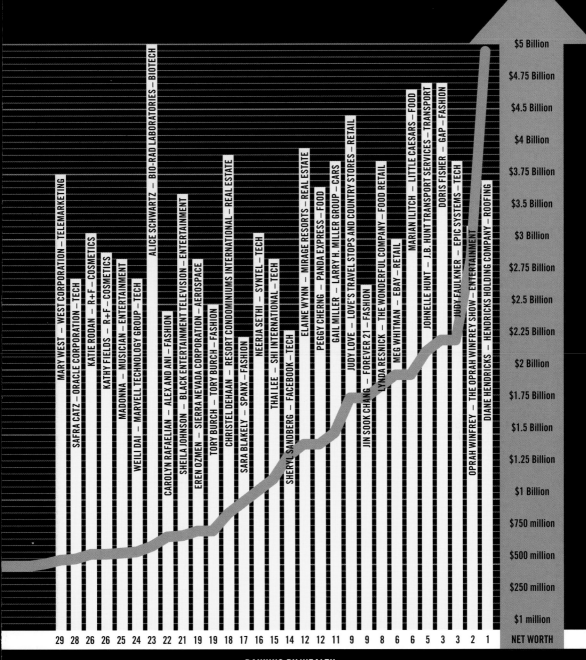

RANKING BY WEALTH

the devotion to work scotched any press mutterings about the couple being out to benefit in column inches from their union.

So the media found themselves spinning somewhere between frustration, confusion and respect. It wasn't until November that Beyoncé issued a few words on the subject, telling *Essence* magazine that she hadn't wanted a big hullabaloo. 'It's been my day so many days already,' she said, perhaps hinting that Jay-Z had made big romantic gestures on previous occasions, though she wasn't giving any details. She hadn't even had an engagement ring. 'It's just material,' she shrugged. 'It's just silly to me.' Her refreshing attitude reaffirmed that any cries of gold-digger – some of which had hung about her after songs such as 'Bills, Bills, Bills' – were embarrassingly off the mark. She was at least spotted with a wedding ring – particularly appropriate given the theme of the next hit that was about to land …

In previous years she'd had to laugh off all manner of overly imaginative internet rumours about their wedding. A favourite was that she'd bought the late Princess Diana's 1981 wedding dress. 'Fabulous!' chuckled Beyoncé in *USA Today*. 'Somebody is so creative! They should plan weddings, they have a great one planned for us! They even have a menu with caviar, and I don't even like caviar!'

She emphasized that the pair had always felt they were meant for each other, and had developed a comfortable closeness over their many years of courtship. If anyone was upset by their eschewing the glitzy public rituals of a superstar wedding, she told Oprah Winfrey, she trusted that those who loved them would understand, as 'at the end of the day, it's your day'. She eventually shared a little: her wedding dress could be spotted in home video clips visible in her 2011 promo for a live version of 'I Was Here'. That same year, she spoke to *Harper's Bazaar* of her great respect for Jay-Z, and confided, 'We focused three years on our marriage and found that it brought us an even stronger bond and connection. But like anything great and successful in your life, marriage takes hard work and sacrifice. It has to be something both you and your husband deeply want.'

It seemed she was growing increasingly comfortable with admitting natural human insecurity, which people could relate to in tandem with her own artistic development into a fiercer, more armoured female force. With a blend of maturity and candour, she enlarged on this. 'The best thing about marriage is the amount of growth you have because you can no longer hide from your fears and insecurities. There's someone right there calling you out on your flaws and building you up when you need the support. If you're with the right person, it brings out the best in you.'

She didn't need too much encouragement to bring out her best. The DVD *The Beyoncé Experience Live* was clocking up triple platinum sales. Those who'd missed the tour could see her opening her show by striding through fireworks and hollering, 'Are you ready to be entertained!' It was a command rather than a question. Jay-Z, Kelly and Michelle made guest appearances, with her husband featuring on 'Upgrade U' and her fellow Destiny's Child alumni joining her for the ever relevant 'Survivor'.

Just weeks before her wedding, Beyoncé had realized another dream by performing at the Grammys with her

> **'IF YOU'RE WITH THE RIGHT PERSON, IT BRINGS OUT THE BEST IN YOU.'**

heroine Tina Turner, in what many perceived as a kind of symbolic handing on of the torch. Beyoncé gave Tina an introduction that told her fans as much about her own influences as it did about Ms Turner. 'Sarah Vaughan, Aretha Franklin, Chaka Khan,' she began:

> … historical women who have performed on this very stage. When I was a little girl, I dreamed of being on this stage, but I knew I needed all the right elements. Like the beat of Donna Summer, the spirit of Mahalia Jackson, the jazz of Ella [Fitzgerald] or Nancy [Sinatra] … Lena Horne, Anita Baker, Diana Ross, Gladys [Knight], Janet [Jackson] and the beautiful melodies of Whitney [Houston] … The legacy they have bestowed is simply irreplaceable, but there is one legend who has the essence of all these things: the glamour, the soul, the passion, the strength, the talent. Ladies and gentlemen, stand on your feet and give it up for the Queen!

Tina and Beyoncé, onstage, shook it like they meant it. After the Prince duet, it was another high-profile Grammys coup for Beyoncé – this was Tina's first live show in no less than seven years. They rocked through 'Proud Mary', the old Ike

& Tina hit (a Creedence Clearwater Revival cover), with Tina, then in her late sixties, bringing as much electric energy to the performance as Beyoncé.

While Beyoncé spent much of the year grafting on both her next album and next film, she took a well-earned break in June to sample, as a spectator, the muddy delights of the Glastonbury Festival in England. Jay-Z was headlining to a huge live and TV audience, bringing hip-hop to the rock bastion, his booking having already wound up musical ultra-conservatives, including former Oasis star Noel Gallagher. Naysayers aside, the show was a triumph, and Beyoncé was thrilled. 'I was so proud of him that night,' she said. 'I don't know if I've ever seen him do a better show. He rocked that crowd, showed them what he's about.' It was here that her own desire to play the festival was born. Jay-Z himself would describe his Glastonbury set as 'the death spasms of an old way of thinking', and certainly he and Beyoncé seemed to now embody a bold new approach to popular music.

With timely impact, she released her new capsule of culture. A fresh record, but also a fresh alter ego. Beyoncé's third album, *I Am... Sasha Fierce*, was technically a double album, as it was released as two discs, though only the length of a single one. In it, she officially introduced her new persona to the masses. 'Sasha Fierce is,' she declared, 'the fun, more sensual, more aggressive, more outspoken and more glamorous

**'SASHA FIERCE IS THE FUN, MORE SENSUAL, MORE AGGRESSIVE, MORE OUTSPOKEN AND MORE GLAMOROUS SIDE THAT COMES OUT WHEN I'M ON THE STAGE.'**

side that comes out when I'm on the stage.' The first disc, *I Am...*, was full of more personal ballad-style songs, while the second disc, *Sasha Fierce*, was a barrage of clubby beat-happy dance cuts. Explaining to Oprah that she'd invented Sasha years ago to help boost her confidence onstage, she posited:

**RIGHT:** Beyoncé and Tina Turner perform together at the 50th Annual Grammy Awards in LA, 2008.

It's kind of like doing a movie. When you put on the wig and the clothes, you walk different. It's no different to anyone else – I feel like we all have that kind of thing which takes over. Usually [for me it's] when I hear the chords, put on my stilettos. Like, the moment right before when you're nervous. Then Sasha Fierce appears, and my posture and the way I speak – and everything – becomes different.'

She wanted to reveal more of 'who I am', and that highlighted the fascinating duality that has coloured and deepened much of her career since. Her outlandish ability to embody contradictions was on display here. She simultaneously offered more personal revelations while at the same time freely acknowledging that her new public persona was a conscious creation. It was the work of someone with an almost Bowie-esque facility for playing (and working) with roles but forging from them some underlying or larger truths.

Released in mid-November 2008, *I Am... Sasha Fierce* was another platinum-selling, multiple Grammy-winning triumph. Its modern, edgy side won most praise, keeping her not so much relevant as ahead of the game. Thanking Jay-Z for pushing her to explore her talent further, Beyoncé switched her producer-collaborator choices around a little for this one. For the ballads disc she worked with Kenneth 'Babyface' Edmonds, who had pop credentials for his Bobby Brown, TLC and Toni Braxton hits; Tricky Stewart, who had previously produced Rihanna's chart-topping 'Umbrella'; and rising star Ryan Tedder, lead singer with OneRepublic, who had started to make a name for himself writing and producing tracks for Jennifer Lopez and Whitney Houston, and would later go on to work with Adele. The second side of the

# SASHA FIERCE GETS MARRIED

**BELOW:** Beyoncé at the BET Awards
2009 in Los Angeles, California.

# I AM… *Sasha Fierce*

Beyoncé famously 'killed off' her alter ego
Sasha Fierce in 2010, once she'd outlived her
usefulness. Beyoncé has said that she adopted
the Sasha Fierce persona as a counterpoint
to her own naturally shy nature, to boost her
courage and sensuality onstage. Once she could
merge the two sides of her personality, she no
longer needed Sasha. But Bey is not the only
female singer with an alter ego. Here
are another famous five.

| BEYONCÉ | SASHA FIERCE |
| --- | --- |

| LADY GAGA | JO CALDERONE |
| --- | --- |

| MARY J. BLIGE | BROOK LYNN |
| --- | --- |

| NICKI MINAJ | ROMAN ZOLANSKI |
| --- | --- |

| MADONNA | ESTHER |
| --- | --- |

| LAURIE ANDERSON | FENWAY BERGAMOT |
| --- | --- |

album was fired up by the likes of Sean Garrett, who had a reputation for creating number one hits for artists such as Usher, Ciara and Janet Jackson, and Rodney Jerkins, who was once again brought on board. However, Mathew Knowles and Beyoncé were still credited as executive producers. But whereas previous works had been effectively and successfully hot-housed, Beyoncé's new status as multi-platform entertainer meant that sessions were spread out over eight months, and over a catalogue of different studios. It's said that as many as seventy tracks were tried out. Recording locations ranged across Atlanta, New York, Miami Beach, Ibiza, Burbank and LA.

Not for the first time, Beyoncé's pitch was broad. 'One side has songs that are more mainstream and another has my more traditional R&B songs for the fans who've been there the whole time,' she told *Billboard*. 'Some of it sounds like Barbra Streisand, Karen Carpenter and The Beatles.'

If that suggested easy listening, that was just one side of the coin. There was a swelling confessional, diary-like nature to some passages, a feature that would increase greatly in her later work. Again, she displayed strength and confidence through admitting to human vulnerability. 'I'm a human being,' she elaborated on another occasion. 'My feelings get hurt. I get scared and nervous like everyone else. And I wanted to show that about myself.

## 'I'M A HUMAN BEING … MY FEELINGS GET HURT. I GET SCARED AND NERVOUS LIKE EVERYONE ELSE.'

The album's about love. I'm a woman, I'm married, and this portion of my life is all in the album. It's a LOT more personal. I'm very private and I don't talk about a lot of things, but there are certain songs on the album that are VERY personal.'

Arguably the most instantly arresting lyrics on the album are from 'If I Were a Boy'. It takes two views of manhood, looking at a boyfriend who likes to 'drink beer with guys' and takes his girlfriend for granted; and then imagining instead a man who would try to 'understand how it feels to love a girl'. This and 'Single Ladies (Put a Ring on It)' were the two biggest hits from *I Am... Sasha Fierce*, with choices for subsequent singles varying for different territories. 'Halo' (which broke records for chart longevity), 'Sweet Dreams', 'Diva', 'Ego', 'Broken-Hearted Girl', 'Video Phone' and 'Why Don't You Love Me?' all got an outing in different regions. With the album selling half a million in its first week in the

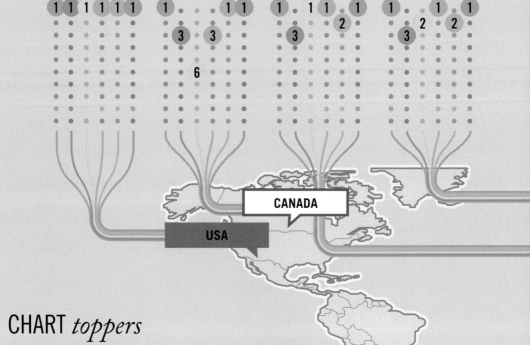

CANADA

USA

# CHART *toppers*

There's no doubt that every album Beyoncé releases
storms the charts, but how does each album's success
compare across the world in terms of chart position and
sales and how does each album compare to the one
before it? *Lemonade* looks to be setting a new record for
Bey, charting as high or higher than her previous albums
in seven out of ten territories.

| ALBUM | Dangerously in Love | B'day | I Am... Sasha Fierce | 4 | Beyoncé | Lemonade |
|---|---|---|---|---|---|---|
| Release date (month, year) | June 2003 | August 2006 | November 2008 | June 2011 | December 2013 | April 2016 |
| WORLD SALES (in million) | 11 | 8 | 8 | 5 | 3 | 1.6 |

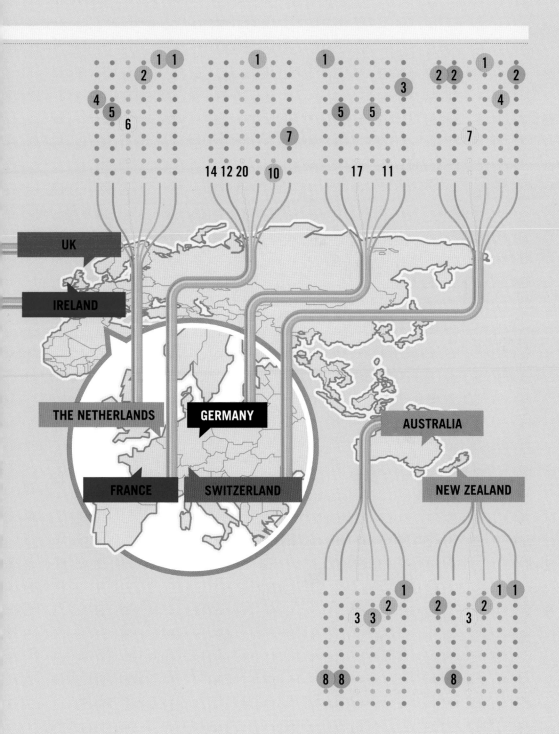

US, and selling an additional million over the following five weeks, she became just the third female artist of that decade to top the Billboard chart with her first three albums. The astutely measured series of targeted singles releases extended its lifespan: it was the second best American seller of the following year, 2009, and now claims to have passed the three million mark in the States, and eight million worldwide. In the UK, it's still her biggest to date. She wasn't too proud to put the hard miles in and promote, performing on a wide range of US TV programmes, from *The Oprah Winfrey Show* to *Saturday Night Live*, and showing up on UK TV in *The X Factor* to duet with winner Alexandra Burke.

Probably Sasha Fierce's most universally loved calling card was 'Single Ladies (Put a Ring on It)', which captured the public imagination as a high-temperature hybrid of dance-floor classic, video gem, sly reference to her own marriage and peculiar neo-feminist anthem. It slid nicely into the category of Beyoncé's strong, sassy sisterhood songs. Some thought it advocated marriage as every girl's dream, reading its message as being: if your boyfriend doesn't propose and put a ring on your finger, tell him to take a hike. But others saw it as a more straightforward rallying cry for commitment, telling men to make their minds up, put a flag in the ground and stick with the good thing they'd found. Either way, it brooked no nonsense. It entered the popular pantheon: some women punching the air, others questioning its priorities. Defenders pointed out that its ultimate focus wasn't on getting him to propose, but on moving on sharply if he didn't.

The video, and her much-imitated, wow-factor, attitude-laden dance moves, finessed the point. And by 'much imitated', we mean even Justin Timberlake spoofed it, sporting a black leotard on a *Saturday Night Live* sketch. It went viral almost before 'going viral' was even a thing. A dance craze ensued, catching on around the world. At the same time, those feminists choosing to embrace its message adopted it as a cause célèbre. *Jezebel* reported on a performance artist, Nina Millin, who recited its lyrics as an empowering dramatic monologue, while years later, in 2016, its resonance was still so high that Michelle Obama chose it, mixing comedy and sincerity, for her impressive, globally watched 'carpool karaoke' session on James Corden's *Late Late Show*.

Of the song's original video, directed by her go-to guy Jake Nava and choreographed by Frank Gatson and JaQuel Knight, Beyoncé stated that a Bob Fosse influence was the key spark. 'I saw this video on YouTube of three dancers, and one of them was Bob Fosse's wife, a choreographer, and they're doing "Walk It Out". It's from the Sixties, one take, and black and white. I thought: wow, how amazing would that be now, because videos have so many different cuts and takes, to just see a non-stop dance video, one take, all the way through?' It was a challenge though. 'It was the most tiring thing I've ever done in my life,' said the renowned workaholic. She and the two other dancers shot the unforgettable result over twelve hours, leaving a long-living legacy. The song went on to win Grammys for Song of the Year, Best R&B Song and Best Female R&B Vocal Performance. The World Music Awards voted it World's Best Single … for 2010.

And it received even more publicity at the MTV Video Music Awards when it *didn't* win. The Best Female Video Award went to Taylor Swift for 'You Belong With Me', but as she was going about her business being presented with the trophy by Shakira and Taylor Lautner, Kanye West infamously gate-crashed the stage, announcing, 'Yo, Tay, I'm really happy for you and I'm gonna let you finish, but Beyoncé had one of the best videos of all time!' As it happens, the overall Video of the Year Award was subsequently given to 'Single Ladies', and Beyoncé – who'd looked aghast at Kanye's narcissistic interruption – invited Taylor Swift back up on stage to 'have her moment'. It was a graceful response that saved an otherwise awkward situation.

> 'IT WAS THE MOST TIRING THING I'VE EVER DONE IN MY LIFE.'

Another talking point was the 'Video Phone' video, which saw Beyoncé and Lady Gaga teaming up as 'bad girls', complete with guns and costume changes galore. Here fans again bore witness to Knowles' bold willingness to take her malleable image anywhere, to gain an added edge by association with then-zeitgeist-surfing artists, and to keep on pushing back the boundaries of what she was expected or 'supposed' to do. Director Hype Williams paid a twisted homage in the video to Tarantino's *Reservoir Dogs*, and Beyoncé also got to fire a bow and arrow, straddle a motorbike and impersonate vintage pin-up Bettie Page. She'd long since left her comfort zone. The lyrics might have shocked the timid: 'You want me naked? If you like this position you can tape it,' she breathed, no longer a goody-goody. Yet she was also demonstrating that playing 'the married woman' didn't mean collapsing inwardly into a tried and trusted, conservative category, a

# HIT ALBUM: *I Am... Sasha Fierce*

In her third solo album, Beyoncé juxtaposes the 'real' her, and her alter ego, stage diva Sasha Fierce. More experimental than her previous albums, *I Am... Sasha Fierce* showcased one of her most iconic singles 'Single Ladies (Put a Ring on It)', while also celebrating her softer side with the more emotive hit single 'If I Were a Boy'.

**World Music Awards**
Best Single **SL**

**Urban Music Awards**
Best Single **H**

**UK Music Video Awards**
Best Pop Video **SL**    Best International Video **D**

**Teen Choice Awards**
Choice Music Album: Female

**Teen Choice Awards**
Choice Music: R&B Track **SL**
Choice Music: Love Song **H**

**Soul Train Music Awards**
Album of the Year

**Soul Train Music Awards**
Song of the Year **SL**

**ALBUM: I AM... SASHA FIERCE**

**NRJ Music Awards**
International Album of the Year

**Nickelodeon Kids' Choice Awards**
Favorite Song **SL**

**NAACP Image Awards**
Outstanding Music Video **IIWB**
Outstanding Music Video **SL**
Outstanding Song **SL**
Outstanding Music Video **WdYL**

**NAACP Image Awards**
Outstanding Album

**MuchMusic Video Awards**
Best Watched Video **WdYL**    Best International Artist Video **SL**

**MTV Video Music Awards Japan**
Best Collaboration **VPe**    Best Female Video **IIWB**

**MTV Europe Music Awards**
Best Video **SL**    Best Song **H**

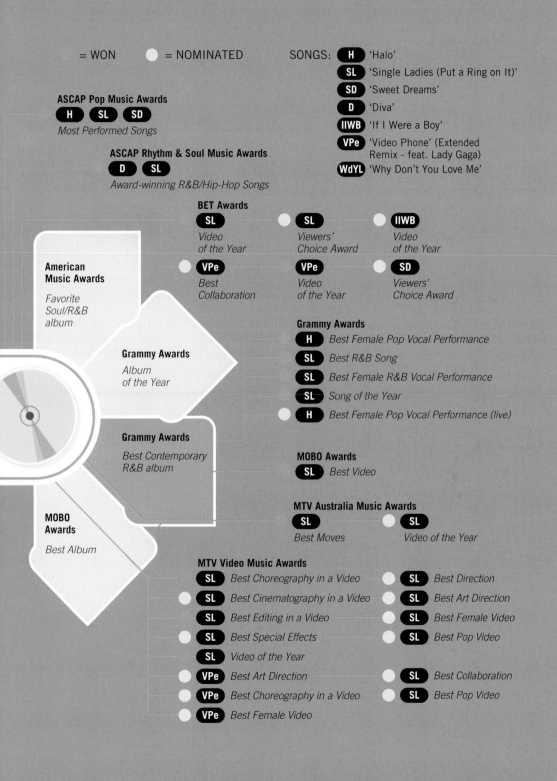

= WON ○ = NOMINATED

SONGS:
**H** 'Halo'
**SL** 'Single Ladies (Put a Ring on It)'
**SD** 'Sweet Dreams'
**D** 'Diva'
**IIWB** 'If I Were a Boy'
**VPe** 'Video Phone' (Extended Remix - feat. Lady Gaga)
**WdYL** 'Why Don't You Love Me'

**ASCAP Pop Music Awards**
**H** **SL** **SD**
*Most Performed Songs*

**ASCAP Rhythm & Soul Music Awards**
**D** **SL**
*Award-winning R&B/Hip-Hop Songs*

**BET Awards**
**SL** *Video of the Year*
○ **SL** *Viewers' Choice Award*
○ **IIWB** *Video of the Year*

○ **VPe** *Best Collaboration*
**VPe** *Video of the Year*
○ **SD** *Viewers' Choice Award*

**American Music Awards**
*Favorite Soul/R&B album*

**Grammy Awards**
*Album of the Year*

**Grammy Awards**
**H** *Best Female Pop Vocal Performance*
**SL** *Best R&B Song*
**SL** *Best Female R&B Vocal Performance*
**SL** *Song of the Year*
○ **H** *Best Female Pop Vocal Performance (live)*

**Grammy Awards**
*Best Contemporary R&B album*

**MOBO Awards**
**SL** *Best Video*

**MOBO Awards**
*Best Album*

**MTV Australia Music Awards**
**SL** *Best Moves*
○ **SL** *Video of the Year*

**MTV Video Music Awards**
**SL** *Best Choreography in a Video*
○ **SL** *Best Cinematography in a Video*
**SL** *Best Editing in a Video*
○ **SL** *Best Special Effects*
**SL** *Video of the Year*
○ **VPe** *Best Art Direction*
○ **VPe** *Best Choreography in a Video*
○ **VPe** *Best Female Video*

○ **SL** *Best Direction*
○ **SL** *Best Art Direction*
○ **SL** *Best Female Video*
○ **SL** *Best Pop Video*
○ **SL** *Best Collaboration*
○ **SL** *Best Pop Video*

theme she was often to return to. Marriage, you might deduce, had changed her, but not in the ways we might assume.

The usually flamboyant Gaga seemed almost sedate by comparison, Beyoncé cleverly borrowing her perceived outrageousness. In fact it seemed that Gaga had gladly accepted to play second fiddle, or even fan-girl, here. She told MTV, 'What I was excited about with Beyoncé is, I had no ego. Neither of us had an ego. It wasn't about competition. It was about: man, let's give the world what they want. Let's do a real girl power collaboration where we support one another.'

Gaga added that she'd wanted to pay tribute to Beyoncé in the video, and even to dress up like her. 'I had Beyoncé hair, and we wore similar outfits.'

As Gaga correctly noted, this was an era in Beyoncé's career where 'she redefined herself aesthetically'. Beyoncé could try out new images for size, without worrying about dull consistency, because her fans were seeing multiple personas within her that resonated within them emotionally and aesthetically and coaxed a response.

**LEFT:** Beyoncé performs her iconic 'Single Ladies' dance at the 2009 MTV Video Music Awards in New York.

The dressings in such videos were the latest flesh on the mythology, but the strong spine was always the indomitable Beyoncé. Gaga concludes, 'It should be applauded that a woman [does] that. She's so great at what she does.'

While the aesthetic redefinition was working out well, Beyoncé was still taking care of the bread-and-butter business, as the I Am… World Tour roared into gear. Not that much about this showbiz extravaganza could be accurately described as 'bread-and-butter'. Launching in March 2009 and running for almost a year, it took in multiple continents (North and South America, Europe, Asia, Africa, Australia) over 108 shows. Rehearsals began eight months before kick-off, and twelve-hour days were not uncommon. French fashion star Thierry Mugler was hired as main costume designer. Beyoncé described him as 'an icon and a legend, and I'm a fan'. He cited the key words: 'Feminine. Free. Warrior. Fierce.' Fashion critics' comments ranged from 'Barbarella on a safari' to 'her costumes were as sparkling as her personality – from NYPD cop, to bride, to Wonder Woman and beyond, the outfits showed off every inch of her perfectly toned body'. If some of these raves read as objectification or ogling, the star was perfectly comfortable now with being loud, unreserved, sexual and untethered: again, fans breathed in the sheer empowerment of it. However, this celebrated new identity wasn't warmly received everywhere, the intended Malaysia concert had to be postponed, as Islamic conservatives feared it would be 'immoral and unclean'. Beyoncé was already far deeper into the twenty-first century of feminism than they were.

Musically, the set promoted the latest album but also incorporated greatest hits (opening with 'Crazy in Love') and still found space for a sweetly nostalgic Destiny's Child medley. 'Single Ladies' and 'Halo' now served as the new climax. Capturing much attention too was Beyoncé's version of the classic love song 'At Last', previously recorded by Etta James. Written as far back as 1941, the soaring number had been given a fresh lease of life for a new generation by Beyoncé singing it in her latest film, *Cadillac Records*, which was to be released as 2008 ended. And when, as 2009 began, she sang it for the newly inaugurated President Obama, the artist sometimes known as Sasha Fierce nailed another moment of indelible pop-cultural history. Yes she could.

**RIGHT:** Beyoncé on the opening night of her 2009 I Am… World Tour in New York.

# SINGLE *ladies*

Not only did the song 'Single Ladies (Put a Ring on It)' become an anthem for women the world over in 2009, but Beyoncé's iconic dance moves became some of the most imitated of all time. Here are the top three moves along with their repetition.

8

6

10

*Biggest group dance of Single Ladies*

100

# BEYONCÉ AT LAST

O ver the course of the 2008 US presidential election campaign, Beyoncé had often been vocally supportive of Chicago senator Barack Obama, even wearing an Obama T-shirt. Nearly half a century since the passing of the Civil Rights Act, there was a general sense that the US was finally ready for (and overdue) its first ever black president. Obama had inspired an entire generation, and Beyoncé was among them. 'I'm really proud,' Beyoncé said openly. 'I think we're making a lot of progress. It's an exciting time for my generation, regardless of whether you're African-American or not.' And, on 4 November 2008, Obama won the election, beating Republican candidate John McCain and his controversial running mate Sarah Palin. He gathered the largest percentage of the vote for a Democrat since Lyndon B. Johnson in 1964, and won more than double the electoral votes of McCain. Change? Hope? Yes we can.

Destiny's Child had performed for George W. Bush all those years ago, but, whereas that had been a pragmatic, professional engagement, this time the politics were personal. And Beyoncé was at the very centre of the Obama celebrations. She even cut short another promo trip to be there, despite the release of *I Am… Sasha Fierce* being scheduled for ten days later. Her sincerity could scarcely be doubted. 'My father grew up in Gadsden, Alabama,' she explained to Piers Morgan on CNN. 'He was escorted to school every day because he was one of the first African-Americans in his class.' Mathew and Tina were both of course immensely proud when their eldest daughter was asked to sing at the Neighborhood Inaugural Ball celebration, which followed the official presidential inauguration ceremony in Washington, DC on 20 January 2009. Her rendition of 'At Last', which she'd sung to Grammy-winning effect in *Cadillac Records*, was the song choice as, historically and memorably, President Barack and First Lady Michelle Obama took their first dance.

**LEFT:** Beyoncé performs 'At Last' at the first Inaugural Ball in Washington, 2009, as the newly elected President Obama and his wife dance.

# RISE *up*

Beyoncé's incredible vocal range compares with some of the all-time female greats.
The graphic below shows her range set against those of various other female artists
where lowest and highest sung keys are represented for each individual, as well as
the song names in which those notes were hit.

## BEYONCÉ

A2 'Party'  E6 'Happy Face'

### Tina Turner

B2 'There'll Always Be Music'  'River Deep Mountain High' G6

### Christina Aguilera

C3 'I Got Trouble'  'The Christmas Song' C#7

### Nina Simone

E2 'Ne Me Quitte Pas'  A5 'Stop'

### Miley Cyrus

B2 'We Can't Stop'  E6 'Just a Girl'

### Aretha Franklin

G2 'I Knew You Were Waiting (For Me)'  B5 'Think'

### Annie Lennox

G2 'Coloured Bedspread'  B5 'There Must Be an Angel'

### Rihanna

B2 'Te Amo'  C#6 'Nobody's Business'

### Lady Gaga

Bb2 'Sexxx Dreams'  B5 'Fancy Pants'

Mariah Carey
F2 'Sweetheart'  'Emotions' G7

Janis Joplin
B2 'Mercedes Benz'  B5 'Try (Just a Little Bit Harder)'

Whitney Houston
C#3 'I Learned from the Best'  'I Wanna Dance with Somebody' C6

Adele
C3 'He Won't Go'  B5 'Melt My Heart to Stone'

Björk
E3 'Pluto'  D6 'Scatterheart'

Dolly Parton
E3 'Backwoods Barbie'  D6 'Mule Skinner Blues'

Joni Mitchell
C#3 'No Apologies'  A5 'Car on a Hill'

Alicia Keys
Bb2 'How to Save a Life'  F#5 'Another Way to Die'

Stevie Nicks
B2 'God's Garden'  E5 'Sisters of the Moon'

Karen Carpenter
D3 'Song for You'  F5 'I'll Never Fall in Love Again'

Taylor Swift
E3 'Begin Again'  F#5 'You Belong with Me'

'I can't even describe to you how I felt,' Beyoncé beamed to *Good Morning America* after serenading the new First Couple. 'I'm actually right now fighting back tears because it's just so emotional. I'm just so proud of my country. This man was born for this. He was born to lead us, and I just feel so inspired and so proud.' The usually impeccably professional Beyoncé clearly struggled to contain her feelings. 'I'm sorry, I'm so embarrassed … I'm just so lucky to be a part of this history. It's probably the most important day of my life, and I'm so grateful.'

The friendship between the Obamas and the Carters was to endure happily. Even back then Barack Obama, no slouch at carrying a tune himself as his love of Al Green and B.B. King songs has testified, was proving his grooviness by telling a radio show that, 'On my iPod, I've got a little bit of Jay-Z and a little bit of Beyoncé. Some of that stuff. I don't want to pretend that I know as much as my young daughters!'

He may well have been interested in the musical background of the first of Beyoncé's two movies of this period too. *Cadillac Records*, directed by Darnell Martin, had only recently come out on 5 December 2008, and *Obsessed*, a thriller, opened in cinemas just four months later. Beyoncé was considered box-office gold.

*Cadillac Records* is often described as an 'Etta James biopic', with Beyoncé in the role of the singer, but it has ambitions to be more than that. It explores the Blues-and-Soul (and Rock'n'Roll) black music scene from the Forties through to the late Sixties. The story chronicles the bumpy life ride of Leonard Chess, the (Polish-Jewish immigrant) pioneering Chicago record-industry boss, and the artists who sang for his Chess Records label. With Oscar-winning actor Adrien Brody as Chess, it gives us Jeffrey Wright as Muddy Waters, Cedric the Entertainer as narrator Willie Dixon, Mos Def as Chuck Berry, Columbus Short as Little Walter and Eamonn Walker as Howlin' Wolf, in addition to Beyoncé as Etta James. Esteemed reviewer Roger Ebert reckoned that 'the film is a fascinating record of the evolution of a black musical style, and the tangled motives of the white men who had an instinct for it'.

Eager to do Etta James justice, Beyoncé studied her life. For some of this, she may not have had to look too far from her own path: James had begun singing in church, then formed a three-girl group, then gone solo. You can see why Knowles related. But then James' story had become more turbulent. On tour with Little Richard in the Fifties, she'd succumbed to heroin addiction. Beyoncé didn't flinch. A stranger to drugs, she visited a Brooklyn rehab centre to try to get a feel for the milieu. She was dedicated to her research, even if it was difficult. She found what she witnessed tough to take. 'I never tried drugs in my life,' she said, 'so I didn't know about it all. It was hard to go there. I learned a lot about life, and about myself.' She saw this – a genuine acting stretch of the kind she'd wanted – as a welcome opportunity to keep surprising her audience. Plus, she still got to sing. She told one interviewer that it was the first film role where she'd felt 'that out-of-body experience that I feel onstage'.

Etta James was reportedly peeved at not being invited to sing 'At Last' for President Obama herself, but the septuagenarian regrouped to be photographed embracing the twenty-seven-year-old Beyoncé at the film's premiere. The younger star reported that Etta told her, 'I loved you from the first time you sung.' Sadly, James died of complications from Alzheimer's disease in 2012. *Rolling Stone* ranked her as twenty-second on its list of the hundred greatest singers of all time.

For all the due diligence and dutiful homework, Beyoncé's manic schedule allowed her just one week for shooting *Cadillac Records*. Yet the director, if concerned beforehand, swiftly became a Knowles' fan. '[I thought] I only have her for six days, how is that going to work?' Darnell Martin told Cinemablend. com. 'Well, how it happens is … everything you imagine this glamorous, iconic, becoming-a-legend woman must be like on set is … simply not true. She's the most down-to-earth, sunshine in my life, wonderful, incredible, easy, brilliant, excited about working, tireless angel.' A shame, then, that the film – in which the music performances were much praised – did not perform as well as hoped at the box office, although Beyoncé's 'captivating' voice won more plaudits and she won a Satellite Award nomination. The soundtrack album, which topped the US Billboard Blues chart, received a 2010 Grammy nomination, as did one of Beyoncé's five songs, 'Once in a Lifetime', which was also Golden Globe nominated. Her soulful rendition of 'I'd Rather Go Blind' was another standout moment, and she proved her sincerity by donating her fee to the drug and alcohol rehabilitation centre Phoenix House.

*Obsessed* may have been arguably a less worthy subject and film, but this thriller struck more of a chord with casual cinema-goers, who enjoyed watching Beyoncé competing for up-and-coming heart-throb Idris Elba. The April 2009 release from Steve Shill, a British TV director who'd moved to the States and worked on *The Sopranos*, *The Wire* and *Deadwood*, told a familiar *Fatal Attraction*-style story. Lisa (Ali Larter) is an office temp who tries everything she can to seduce her boss, Derek (Elba), eventually taking advantage of him when he's insensibly drunk. When Derek's wife, Sharon (Beyoncé), suspects an affair, she kicks her husband out, but then, months later, when the couple have reconciled, deranged stalker Lisa breaks into their house. It boils down to a mortal fight between the two women which – spoiler alert – Beyoncé wins.

What attracted Beyoncé to this potboiler? She herself had earlier stated that she wanted to play a role that had nothing to do with the music industry – perhaps the appeal lay in taking on a new challenge. She concentrated, she said, on 'the emotion and the psychology of the relationship'. As for those punch-up, hair-pulling, fisticuffs scenes, she found the training not that different to dance moves. The let's-rumble finale took a week to film, as long as her entire shift on *Cadillac Records*. The film did well,

> '**I NEVER TRIED DRUGS IN MY LIFE, SO I DIDN'T KNOW ABOUT IT ALL. IT WAS HARD TO GO THERE. I LEARNED A LOT ABOUT LIFE, AND ABOUT MYSELF.**'

despite being less than glowingly reviewed. That epic climactic catfight developed a cult notoriety and even won Best Fight at the MTV Movie Awards. 'We went for it,' laughed Ali Larter. 'We were going: you clock, I clock. A little head-butting, get some kicks in there. Over a week of it, we got bruised up.' Also rather bruising was Beyoncé's nomination as Worst Actress at the 2010 Razzies, though she seemed to take it in good-tempered stride, perhaps secure and confident in the acting skills she'd so clearly demonstrated in other, more nuanced projects.

**LEFT:** Beyoncé performs at the Condé Nast Media Group's Fifth Annual Fashion Rocks at Radio City Music Hall, New York in 2008.

No matter: she was back to her habitual winning ways at the January 2010 Grammy Awards. She received ten nominations, including those for *I Am... Sasha Fierce*, 'Halo' and 'Single Ladies', the latter picking up Song of the Year. Winning six, she broke the record for most awards in one night by a female artist, despite her album being pipped to the prize by Taylor Swift's. She also performed, singing 'If I Were a Boy' and Alanis Morissette's 'You Oughta Know'. The ceremony featured a tribute to the deceased Michael Jackson, and was opened by Lady Gaga and Elton John. This was an indication of how high Gaga's star was soaring at this time, and another duet with Beyoncé was arranged that combined the two women's star status. Technically, this time it was Beyoncé who was guesting with Gaga. 'Telephone' was the sixth number one for both acts, and its nine-minute video – or short film – was the real talking point, a huge pop culture event and the coming together of two female icons.

Swedish director Jonas Åkerlund had been the hottest of video gurus since Madonna's 'Ray of Light', and his eye-popping colours here made a powerful impact, as the film referenced a catholic range of influences and sources, such as Russ Meyer, Tarantino's *Kill Bill* and *Pulp Fiction* and Ridley Scott's *Thelma & Louise*. Gaga had originally written the song (with Rodney Jerkins) for Britney Spears to guest on, but Spears passed. Gaga told MTV that the nagging, insistent telephone in question is a voice in her head, telling her to keep working, harder and harder. 'That's my fear – that the phone's ringing, my head's ringing – it's just the thoughts in your head, that's another fear.' So with true physical self-affirmation and a refusal to jump to anyone's beat but their own, the two ladies express a preference to hit the dance floor and escape – a traditional pop metaphor for living actively rather than passively – rather than respond to those bugaboo calls. In the age of growing 24/7 online communication, it resonated.

That video, though. Beyoncé has rarely been so bad-ass. Here, nicknamed Honey Bee, she bails Gaga out of jail. They then go to a diner where they (rather harshly, if you don't suspend disbelief) poison the other guests, then drive away in the 'Pussy Wagon' as wanted murderers and targets of a high-speed police car chase. The gaudy but genuinely surreal imagery doubled down on the fresh edge to Beyoncé, who was happy to show she was just as sassy and risk-taking as the new girl in town. Gaga elaborated on what she described as the 'Tarantino-inspired quality' of the video. She and Tarantino were 'having lunch one day', she said, 'and I was explaining the concept for the video … he said "You gotta use the Pussy Wagon [which Uma Thurman drove in *Kill Bill*]", and he lent it to us.' She later nailed the video's impact, saying, 'What I like about it is it's a real, true, pop event. When I was younger, I was always excited when there was a big giant event happening in pop music, and that's what I wanted this to be.' Amy Odell observed in *New York* magazine, 'This is Gaga's video, but Beyoncé is the best part. She actually shows the angry, crazy side that we just knew lurked beneath her too-perfect façade.' If there had been a minority of critics who had still felt Beyoncé's image was too squeaky clean, this reiterated that they were out of touch and out of line. She'd been moving cleverly away from Destiny's Child's daintier side for some time. She really had taken a bold leap in her last few releases, enacting dynamic departures, and peak pop provocation had been achieved. In 2015 Billboard was to name the tingle-inducing 'Telephone' the best video of the decade so far.

Beyoncé was pleased with the sidestep into yet another character-cum-creation, and generously described Gaga as 'so talented – I'm so happy to work with her, I love her'. Gaga too revealed Beyoncé's dedication, when talking to TV host Ryan Seacrest. 'I mean, can you imagine me saying, "OK now, Beyoncé, you have to call me a very bad girl and feed me a honey bun"? She trusted me because she likes my work, and she knows that I love her and it's a mutual respect. It ended up being a masterpiece because she was so courageous.'

Beyoncé's dancing had by now of course become a source of popular wonder in itself, from the precision-based moves of her early years to the more avant-garde, statement-making steps of her ongoing solo superstar phase. Ashley Everett, the captain of her dance troupe, has spoken of how much work goes into the moves that appear so effortless. To keep up with Beyoncé she cross-trains, and does yoga and Pilates. Rehearsals prior to going on the road can involve gruelling twelve-to-sixteen-hour days. Everett has also revealed that the squad load up on vitamins and use saunas and steam rooms to fight off any bugs or toxins. Beyoncé is a champion of 'body positivity', and Everett's confirmed that 'she's all about women empowerment and she just loves beautiful people inside and out. Whether you're thin, thick, short or tall, it's really positive because she has all these types of women on her tour. I've definitely embraced that we're all different, and that you have to love your body from the inside out.'

# BEY AT THE *Grammys*

With a total of twenty-two awards and sixty-two nominations from the Grammy Awards for her music (as a solo artist and with Destiny's Child), Beyoncé is the most nominated woman in Grammy history.

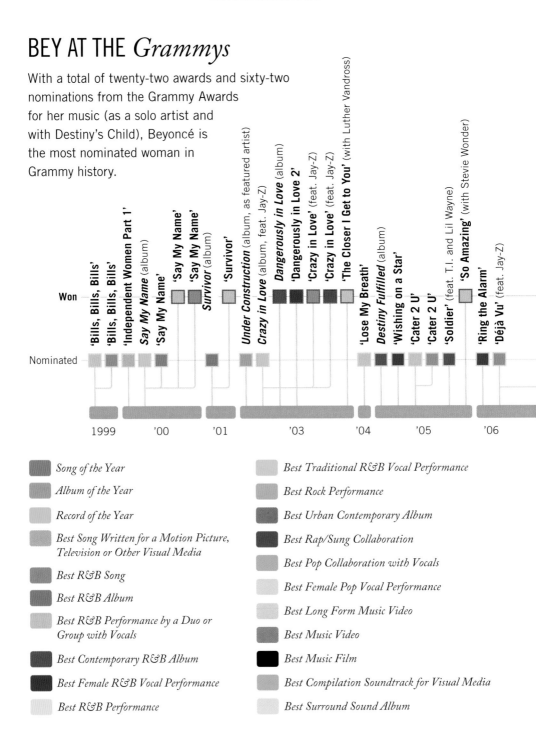

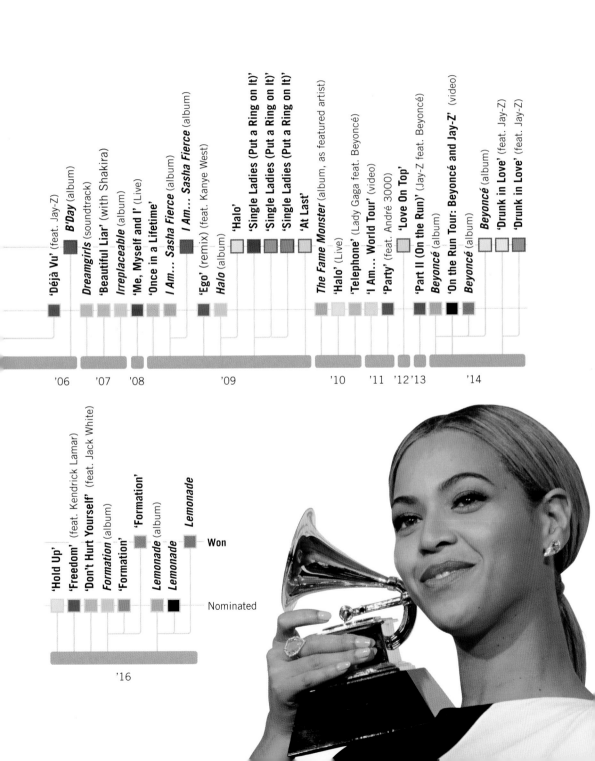

'Déjà Vu' (feat. Jay-Z)
B'Day (album)
Dreamgirls (soundtrack)
'Beautiful Liar' (with Shakira)
Irreplaceable (album)
'Me, Myself and I' (Live)
'Once in a Lifetime'
I Am... Sasha Fierce (album)
I Am... Sasha Fierce (album)
'Ego' (remix) (feat. Kanye West)
Halo (album)
'Halo'
'Single Ladies (Put a Ring on It)'
'Single Ladies (Put a Ring on It)'
'Single Ladies (Put a Ring on It)'
'At Last'
The Fame Monster (album, as featured artist)
'Halo' (Live)
'Telephone' (Lady Gaga feat. Beyoncé)
'I Am... World Tour' (video)
'Party' (feat. André 3000)
'Love On Top'
'Part II (On the Run)' (Jay-Z feat. Beyoncé)
Beyoncé (album)
'On the Run Tour: Beyoncé and Jay-Z' (video)
Beyoncé (album)
'Drunk in Love' (feat. Jay-Z)
'Drunk in Love' (feat. Jay-Z)

'06    '07   '08        '09            '10    '11  '12'13      '14

'Hold Up'
'Freedom' (feat. Kendrick Lamar)
'Don't Hurt Yourself' (feat. Jack White)
Formation (album)
'Formation'
'Formation'
Lemonade (album)
Lemonade

Won

Lemonade

Nominated

'16

The Knowles' workaholic ethic was testing even Beyoncé's effervescent energies, though. Grammy night – the latest in a long line of awards celebrations – had revealed a surprisingly emotional, vulnerable side to the superstar, who was in tears as she accepted her trophy for 'Halo'. 'This has been such an amazing night for me,' she said – but after five high-flying years as a solo artist, she needed a rest. Even Beyoncé gets tired. To the shock of fans and the media she declared that she needed some time out. She felt a desire to take stock and also to take a respite from the music industry carousel. To see something of the world outside the trooper's treadmill. She revealed, 'It's definitely time to take a break, to recharge my batteries. I'd like to take about six months and not go into the studio. I need to just live life, to be inspired by things again.'

Her mother, Tina, had been urging her to take a breather, it transpired. In the end the time off lasted for around nine months. But during this well-earned hiatus, Beyoncé's relationship with her highly motivated father took a painful dent. Her parents' relationship had deteriorated over the years, and, sadly, Tina Knowles had filed for divorce in November 2009, after she and Mathew had been living separately for most of that year. In October, Mathew had been hit with a paternity suit by Alexsandra Wright, a Canadian actress who had appeared in popular TV hospital sitcom *Scrubs*. Her son Nixon, born in 2010, was Beyoncé's half-brother. Wright later saw fit to apologize to Tina, Beyoncé and Solange for 'the pain [she'd] contributed to their lives'.

In March 2011, having taken that time out to reflect, Beyoncé decided her father would no longer act as her manager. It can't have been an easy decision, either personally or professionally, to part ways from the man who'd steered her from childhood competition winner to arguably the world's hottest showbiz property. She released a statement to Associated Press at the time, saying, 'I am grateful for everything he has taught me. He is my father for life and I love my dad dearly. I grew up watching both he [sic] and my mother manage and own their own businesses. They were hard-working entrepreneurs and I will continue to follow in their footsteps.' Whether the decision came as a result of the personal dramas of the preceding year, or simply because Beyoncé's fame had now reached an unprecedented level, which Mathew had less experience of handling, Beyoncé had a sturdy solution to hand. Her mogul husband's Roc Nation entertainment company took the wheel, while Beyoncé from hereon would technically manage herself.

Despite what had clearly been a difficult time, the Knowleses sought to handle their divorce with dignity. Tina and Mathew released a press release, intended to calm the media, which said: 'The decision to end our marriage is an amicable one. We remain friends, parents, and business partners. If anyone is expecting an ugly, messy fight, they will be sadly disappointed. We ask for your respect of our privacy as we handle this matter.' Their divorce was finalized in late 2011. Mathew was remarried, to Gena C. Avery, in 2013, while Tina married actor Richard Lawson in 2015.

**ABOVE:** Jay-Z, Beyoncé and Lady Gaga attend Stevie Wonder: Songs in the Key of Life in California, 2015.

Mathew was, in public at least, understanding of Beyoncé's decision, which echoed those of Kelly Rowland and Michelle Williams, who had dropped him as their solo-career manager the previous year. 'It should come as no surprise that at almost thirty years old she wants to have more control of her own business,' he reasoned. 'Beyoncé, I feel, is the number one artist in the world right now. That's a great feeling, as a father and manager. Business is business and family is family. I love my daughter and am very proud of who she is and all that she has achieved. I look forward to her continued great success.' He would, he added, be concentrating on other areas of his World Music Entertainment roster, not least the gospel division. He's since become a serious player in the marketing of Country music, and children's music too.

So Beyoncé's 'break' so far hadn't been quite as relaxing as she'd maybe hoped. Still, she travelled (as opposed to toured) and saw the world outside of concert stadia. She ignored speculative rumours of a Destiny's Child reunion, enjoyed some sightseeing and some 'married couple' time. 'I enjoyed the simple things like driving and picking my nephew up from school,' she told Piers Morgan. 'Travelling but not working and actually visiting museums and seeing ballets … and having great conversations with the people on the plane.' It may be hard to picture that at this level of stardom Beyoncé opted to fly by any means other than private jet, but she seems to have been genuinely delighted to re-engage with 'normal' life after so long perpetually in the public eye.

> 'SHE'S ALL ABOUT WOMEN EMPOWERMENT AND SHE JUST LOVES BEAUTIFUL PEOPLE INSIDE AND OUT.'
>
> ASHLEY EVERETT, CAPTAIN OF HER DANCE TROUPE

She made up for lost time and relished filling her senses with new sights and experiences, truly seeing the world. She visited the Great Wall of China, the Egyptian pyramids, Europe and Australia, and took in a fair bit of culture, exploring art galleries and restaurants. 'I gave myself a break,' she told

**LEFT:** Beyoncé struts her stuff onstage at the 52nd Annual Grammy Awards, California, 2010.

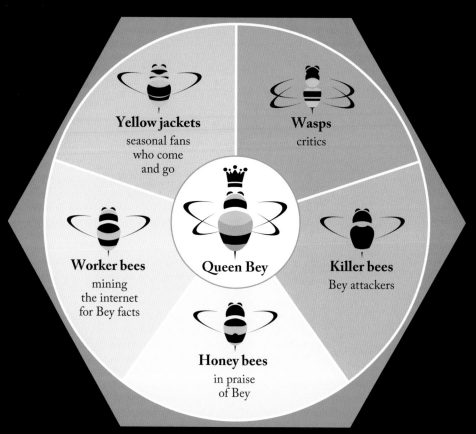

# IN THE *fandom*

Not surprisingly, as one of the most powerful women in the music world, Beyoncé has millions of dedicated followers watching every move and hanging on her slightest utterance. The fans, and the sites they've created to celebrate everything Bey, are legion. Though not yet as numerous as the world's bee population – 6.5 billion.

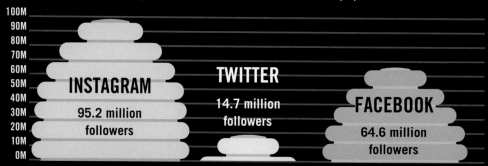

*Cosmopolitan*. 'I took a year off. Now that sounds indulgent, but I'd worked since the age of fifteen, and never taken any time out. My life has always been about next, next, next … always moving on. I just decided to stop.

'It was the best decision I've ever made, and definitely a milestone. I took time out, spent time with my man, my friends, my family. I got to sleep in my own bed night after night, which is a massive thing for me!' Even when she admitted she'd not been entirely off duty, setting up a new production company and learning how to direct and edit a DVD, she smiled, 'What was great was having this normal life of sleeping, getting up, going to an office and then coming home. Coming home is a wonderful thing.'

Of course, for one so professionally driven, it was soon time once again to run the world.

9

# WHO RUNS THE WORLD?

After a year away from the spotlight, when Beyoncé got busy again in 2011, she *really* got busy. That year saw her headlining Glastonbury (the first solo female act to do so in two decades), releasing her fourth consecutive album to debut at number one on the US Billboard chart and – much to the delight of her fans – becoming pregnant. As a sidebar, she won an award from the New York Association of Black Journalists for an article she'd written for *Essence* magazine, discussing her career hiatus. She'd titled it 'Eat, Play, Love'. The appetite of the Renaissance woman, who at one time had admitted 'I just wish I was better at everything', was well and truly reborn.

Jay-Z had won over the doubters at the Glastonbury Festival in 2008. Surely, three years later, people would greet the announcement that Beyoncé, as big a star as existed, was to headline with unanimous whoops and cheers? Apparently not. There were still a few out-of-touch rockers bemoaning the 'pop' invasion of 'their' turf. Largely though, their groans were dismissed. 'She'll make the rest of the bill resemble unwashed sock puppets,' wrote the *Observer's* Barbara Ellen. 'Beyoncé will provide some much-needed glitz,' added the *NME*. 'And will hopefully sing "Crazy in Love" loud enough to drown out the regretful sobs of those who've overdone the meow meow.' The woman herself was looking forward to it: 'Everyone who attends is really appreciative of music and is in such a good mood that entire weekend. I'm pumped just thinking about that audience and soaking up their energy.'

That positivity aside, Beyoncé faced controversy on another front after appearing in 'blackface' costume and make-up in a French magazine as part of a 'tribute' to 'African queens through the ages'. The intention was to help to

**LEFT:** Beyoncé attends the MTV Video Music Awards in Los Angeles, 2011.

promote Jay-Z's investment in a Fela Kuti musical, but it perhaps came across as a rare and uncharacteristic misstep from an artist who was and remains so thoroughly invested in racial equality, a cause she was to champion with growing intensity in subsequent years.

Surviving this and the sticky professional split with her father, Beyoncé was on more unequivocally impressive ground when joining First Lady Michelle Obama and others in a new foundation to combat obesity. 'Let's Move!' was an initiative to 'raise a generation of healthier kids', for which Beyoncé filmed a video and re-recorded her song 'Get Me Bodied' (from *B'Day*) as 'Move Your Body'. She was, she said, 'excited to be part of this effort to address a public health crisis' and was keen to sing Michelle Obama's praises. The feeling was mutual. The First Lady was filmed dancing to the Beyoncé track at a Washington DC school in support of the cause. 'Beyoncé is one of my favourite performers on the planet,' Michelle said. Now that's a quote the singer could use on posters.

The hotly anticipated Glastonbury show on 26 June was intended to coincide with the fourth album's release two days earlier, though before then several tracks had, to her distress, been leaked online. That Sunday night in Somerset, however, in front of a crowd of 175,000 and a massive TV audience, the star was the belle of muddy Britain. The show – an event as much as a show – ensured that she crossed over into every demographic, even the rock fraternity, as if she hadn't already. 'Glastonbury, I want y'all to know right now you are witnessing my dream!' she proclaimed. 'I always wanted to be a rock star and tonight we are all rock stars.' She underlined the point by including a cover of Kings of Leon's 'Sex on Fire' in her set.

Chris Martin of Coldplay had been instrumental in persuading her to play the festival, and his then-wife Gwyneth Paltrow was seen enjoying Beyoncé's set alongside Jay-Z. Beyoncé admitted she'd asked Martin, and U2's Bono, for tips on the venue. 'I'm the biggest fan of U2 and Coldplay,' she said. 'I've spoken to both of them about my set list. Those guys are a little bit more familiar with festivals, and I needed their approval.' Afterwards she basked in the approval of many, many thousands more. 'This night was like a dream,' she said soon after coming offstage, clearly still buzzing. 'I'm just so honoured really – this was the highlight of my career … I don't normally do festivals and I was very nervous! Everyone gave me so much love and I will never, ever, ever forget this night.'

# THE POWER *of 4*

Bey and Jay-Z reckon that the number *4* has been a recurring motif through their lives. Here are some of the ways they have embraced their lucky number and made it count.

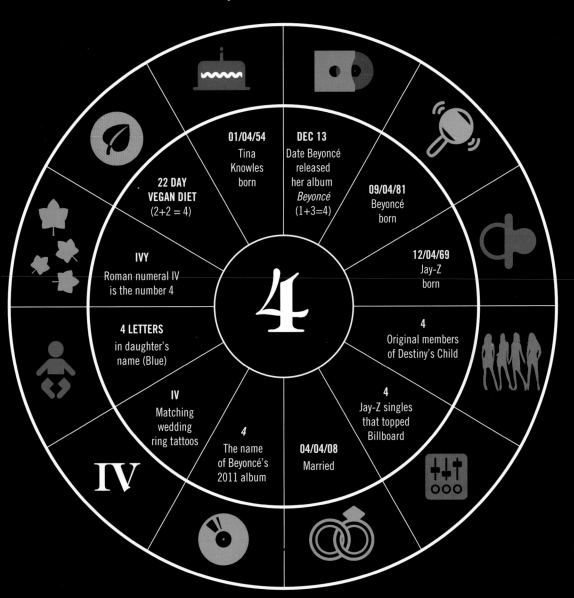

01/04/54
Tina Knowles born

DEC 13
Date Beyoncé released her album *Beyoncé* (1+3=4)

09/04/81
Beyoncé born

22 DAY VEGAN DIET
(2+2 = 4)

IVY
Roman numeral IV is the number 4

12/04/69
Jay-Z born

4 LETTERS
in daughter's name (Blue)

4
Original members of Destiny's Child

IV
Matching wedding ring tattoos

*4*
The name of Beyoncé's 2011 album

04/04/08
Married

4
Jay-Z singles that topped Billboard

4

IV

While a few found the guest spot by Bristol trip-hop enigma Tricky a poor fit, reviews overall were effusive. Even George Michael took to Twitter to say, 'I love that woman. Great writer, artist, singer, person. She just gets better and better.'

The next question was whether that ongoing, relentless improvement would show through on the fourth album, the rather prosaically titled *4*. Whereas subsequent albums would reveal a truly liberated, daring Beyoncé, *4* was slightly less adventurous, perhaps representing a transition point towards these later albums. Beyoncé talked in advance of the album release about much genre-hopping within its boundaries. 'I'm not putting myself in a box,' she promised MTV. 'It's not R&B, it's not typically pop, it's not rock: it's just everything I love all mixed together. My own little gumbo of music.' The unfortunate leaking of tracks undoubtedly irritated her but she responded in public with thoughtful restraint. 'While this is not how I wanted to present my new songs,' she wrote on Facebook, 'I appreciate the positive response from my fans … I make music to make people happy; I appreciate that everyone has been so anxious to hear them …' In retrospect, this turn of events may well have influenced her 'surprise' releases in the following years.

## WATCH ME ON YOUR *video phone*

Every new Beyoncé video explodes on to the music scene when it's released. It comes as no surprise that 'Single Ladies (Put a Ring on It)' is the most watched video of all her tracks on Youtube, with its much imitated dance routine, but this graphic shows the other close runners up. These figures were correct on 2/08/16.

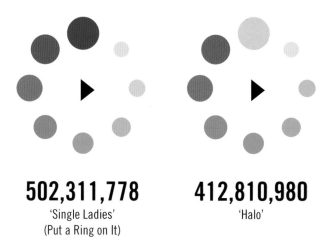

**502,311,778**
'Single Ladies'
(Put a Ring on It)

**412,810,980**
'Halo'

*4* was a mostly slow-tempo, reflective album, the themes of which included self-analysis, female empowerment and harmonious monogamy. Critical responses varied, with some celebrating it as 'accomplished' and others finding it less inspiring than previous offerings. *Rolling Stone* thought it her 'strangest' record. Yet its striving for the personal and intimate – something she'd consistently pursued as a mature artist – truly convinced this time, even if the lyrics didn't always match the insights of those on its predecessor. Perhaps the dazzling lead single, 'Run the World (Girls)', gave a misleading impression of what to expect. Its assertive aggression was, tonally, from another planet to most of the album – and it was unquestionably the most striking moment herein. Unusually for Beyoncé, *4* didn't perform well sales-wise, and it was her first album without a US number one, or even a top-ten hit.

Putting aside sales figures, 'Run the World (Girls)', and especially its video, showed Beyoncé at the top of her form again, once more revisiting the theme of female empowerment. Its electro-flavoured dancehall R&B sampled Major Lazer's 'Pon De Floor' and hammered home its ballistic assertiveness. 'It's … riskier,' she told *Billboard*. 'I heard the track and loved that it was so different: it felt a bit African, electronic, and futuristic. It reminded me of how much I

**374,529,031**
'Drunk in Love'

**321,206,235**
'Run the World' (Girls)

**246,731,022**
'Crazy in Love' ft Jay-Z

love mixing different cultures and eras, things that don't typically go together, to create a new sound.' She added that she always tried to avoid the 'safe' and go against the grain, always setting higher goals than those already achieved.

The Francis Lawrence-directed video utilized no less than eight choreographers and posed Beyoncé in the Mojave Desert in what resembled a post-apocalyptic war zone, wearing a crown and gladiator costume. Her dancers opted for military chic. Beyoncé led her army of women, rode a black horse and saw off a male army. The video was an outrageous menagerie of colourful *Mad Max*-inflected craziness.

That choreography was again a magnet for praise. Beyoncé's long-term creative director Frank Gatson Jr was a key figure in the arrangements for her dance set-ups. He once spoke of how, out of eight hundred girls auditioning for a Super Bowl performance, he'd whittled it down to just a hundred. Then he and Beyoncé would look for the 'professional' and 'magical'. Beyoncé meant business when it came to who she'd be dancing with, he said to *Dance Spirit* magazine, adding, 'She doesn't want watered-down choreography. She'll do almost anything, as long as she remains a lady. She has

> ## 'SHE'S COMPLETELY RELENTLESS IN HER PURSUIT OF PERFECTIONISM.'
> **TODD TOURSO**

class with everything she does, even a booty shake. She knows technique will keep your movement classy. When you mix ballet with street movement, you get the Beyoncé brand. We call it country fried chicken with hot sauce.'

Another member of her creative team, Todd Tourso, has said, 'She's completely relentless in her pursuit of perfection. When you have this kind of leadership and muse and mentor, the sky's the limit.' Beyoncé herself has confided that – like an athlete mastering a sport – she watches her performances back afterwards, and struggles to enjoy the many successes rather than noticing the minuscule faults that can be tweaked or corrected. But while standards were high, she was clearly a sympathetic boss. One dancer recalled a South American show in pouring rain where a few dancers slipped onstage. They anticipated a military-style telling-off, only to see Beyoncé grinning at them, in stitches of laughter.

**LEFT:** Beyoncé performs during a concert in the Rock in Rio Festival, Rio de Janeiro, Brazil, 2013.

She promoted 'Run the World (Girls)' with a buzz-fuelling performance at the *Billboard* Music Awards, yet it couldn't gain her usual traction chart-wise. It topped out at number twenty-nine in the US, and stalled outside the top ten in Britain. As well as a remix EP, other tracks were released as singles through the next year and a half, including '1 + 1', 'Best Thing I Never Had', 'Party', 'Love On Top' and 'Countdown'. While the commercial performance of *4* was formidable by most artists' standards, it left the impression that, despite her creative hiatus, Beyoncé's music was, to a certain degree, treading water, at least in terms of the charts. Little did we then know how radically her next album was going to reboot her sound and image.

But before the next professional step, kicking off a new year, was a huge personal one: the patter of tiny feet. Fans had been playing guessing games in advance as to whether the next generation was on its way. A year earlier, Beyoncé had told an interviewer that she felt self-aware and that thirty was 'the ideal age' for motherhood because enough maturity had been gained in order to have boundaries and standards. 'But you're young enough to be a young woman. I'm so looking forward to it.' It had sounded like a hint to the diva's believers – and now their suspicions were proven right.

Just two months later, the secret was out. After performing 'Love On Top' at the MTV Video Music Awards, Beyoncé pointedly opened her jacket, rubbed her stomach and told her audience, 'I want you to feel the love that's growing inside me.' Incredibly, this became the most tweeted about moment in history to date. After MTV led the pack with 'OMG Beyoncé just made a huge announcement on the #VMA carpet! #baby!!!!!' over eight thousand tweets a second on the subject were clocked around the planet. And the MTV show rapidly became the most watched MTV broadcast of all time. Popular culture was as big as ever!

The world's media were in gooey raptures when Beyoncé and Jay-Z's daughter, Blue Ivy, was born on 7 January 2012, at Manhattan's Lenox Hill Hospital. The happy couple were now so universally famous that, to guarantee privacy for the birth, they had to take over and lock down a whole floor of the hospital, with double security. Yet all went well, and they soon released a statement: 'We are happy to announce the arrival of our beautiful daughter, Blue Ivy Carter. She was delivered naturally at a healthy seven pounds and it was the best experience of both our lives. We are thankful to everyone for all your prayers, well wishes, love and support.' The inner circle tweeted gaily. Sister Solange declared that Blue Ivy was 'the most beautiful girl in the world', while Rihanna tweeted, 'Welcome to the world, princess! Love, Aunty Rih.' Within three weeks, Jay-Z and Beyoncé had patented Blue Ivy's name with the US Patent and Trademark Office.

Jay-Z was quick to express his joy lyrically and musically, through the online release of a new track eulogizing Blue Ivy. A mere two days after his daughter's birth, he gave the world 'Glory', via his website lifeandtimes.com. Yet this was no ordinary parental pride-fest. The track was astonishingly candid and intimate, revealing that the couple had struggled to become pregnant and that, furthermore, Beyoncé had suffered a miscarriage previously. On a happier note, the track revealed that the baby Jay-Z referred to as 'the child of a child from Destiny's Child' had been conceived in Paris, the city of love. The media lapped up this uncharacteristic flood of personal revelations. Blue Ivy, credited as 'B.I.C.', could be heard crying on the track, thus at two days old becoming the youngest person ever to feature on the Billboard chart.

Of course, it wasn't Beyoncé's style to lay low for too long. By early summer, just over five months later, she was back treading the boards, returning to live action with four nights at the opening of the Ovation Hall in Atlantic City. On her website she posted a pragmatic: 'Getting back to business.' She spoke of plans for new albums and films, and, while some turned out to be red herrings (the mooted remake of *A Star Is Born* in which she was to take the lead role hasn't come to fruition yet, although it may soon emerge with different actors involved), by 2013 she was firing on all cylinders again. The *New York Post* reported that Jay-Z, whose Roc Nation was now co-managing her along with giant tour company Live Nation, was firming up the fine print on a deal for her comeback tour. Numbers as unfathomably big as $150 million for her projected earnings were quoted.

But before she could hit the ground running, the public was desperate to hear Beyoncé talk about the baby. US *Vogue* persuaded her to open up in March 2013, as, alongside a 'sexy' (their adjective) lingerie photoshoot emphasizing body confidence and how good she looked so soon after giving birth, she spoke about pregnancy and motherhood. She revealed that at eight months pregnant she'd felt extremely maternal and wondered if it was even possible to bond any more. But then, when she saw her baby, she knew it was. And she wasn't afraid to talk frankly about the experience of childbirth. 'During my labour, I had a very strong connection with my child,' she said. 'I felt like when I was having contractions I envisioned my child pushing through a very heavy door. I imagined this tiny infant doing all the work, so I couldn't think about my own pain. We were talking. I know it sounds crazy, but I felt a communication.' She referred to her daughter as 'my road dog, my homey, my best friend', explaining that her family and closest friends were present when she gave birth, and that 'everything that scared me just was not present in that room. It was the best day of my life.' Pressed, inevitably, on when or whether she'd be having a second child, she confessed that in younger days she'd swung between sometimes wanting four and sometimes wanting none. 'Now I definitely want another … but I don't know when.'

She emphasized the importance of Blue having as normal an upbringing as possible. She wanted her, she said, to 'experience life and run through the sprinklers.

### 'EVERYTHING THAT SCARED ME JUST WAS NOT PRESENT IN THAT ROOM. IT WAS THE BEST DAY OF MY LIFE.'

Have slumber parties, and trust, and live, and do all the things that any child should be able to do.' Defying outmoded social conventions by stressing that she felt even more confident about her body now, and perhaps hinting at the recent recalibration of her family relationships, she added, 'I feel like I'm an adult; I've grown. I don't have to please anyone. I feel free. Heavier, thinner, whatever, I feel a lot more like a woman. More feminine, more sensual, and no shame. I can do what I want, say what I want.' The only note that rang false in the engaging and frank interview was when she discussed calling a halt on her career. 'I can retire if I want – that's why I've worked so hard,' she said. Yes, she'd worked hard. But she wasn't about to retire any time soon.

Quite the contrary. A Destiny's Child ballads compilation, *Love Songs*, did well at the start of 2013. It featured one brand new track, the Pharrell-produced 'Nuclear', and clearly had Beyoncé's blessing: she was 'proud to announce' on her website 'the first new Destiny's Child music in eight years'. No sooner was this

**RIGHT:** Beyoncé rubs her stomach to reveal her pregnancy to fans while onstage at the 2011 MTV Video Music Awards.

# HIT ALBUM: *4*

Playing on the notion that the number '4' has been a lucky talisman in her life, and the fact that this was her fourth album, Beyoncé released *4* in 2011 after a short career break. The album marked her first creative pursuit since her management split with her father, and met with critical acclaim for its mature take on female empowerment and its intimate revelations.

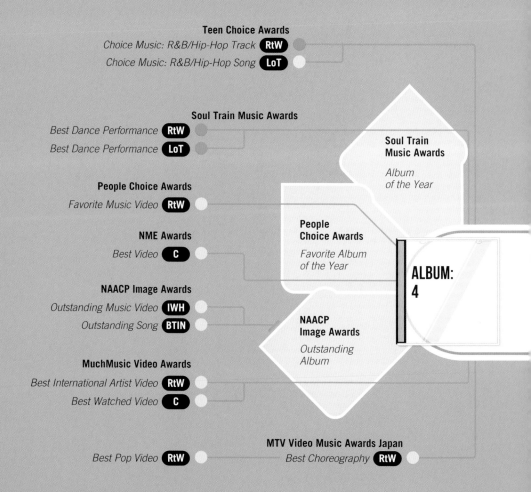

**Teen Choice Awards**

*Choice Music: R&B/Hip-Hop Track* **RtW**

*Choice Music: R&B/Hip-Hop Song* **LoT**

**Soul Train Music Awards**

*Best Dance Performance* **RtW**

*Best Dance Performance* **LoT**

**Soul Train Music Awards**

*Album of the Year*

**People Choice Awards**

*Favorite Music Video* **RtW**

**People Choice Awards**

*Favorite Album of the Year*

**NME Awards**

*Best Video* **C**

**ALBUM: 4**

**NAACP Image Awards**

*Outstanding Music Video* **IWH**

*Outstanding Song* **BTIN**

**NAACP Image Awards**

*Outstanding Album*

**MuchMusic Video Awards**

*Best International Artist Video* **RtW**

*Best Watched Video* **C**

*Best Pop Video* **RtW**

**MTV Video Music Awards Japan**

*Best Choreography* **RtW**

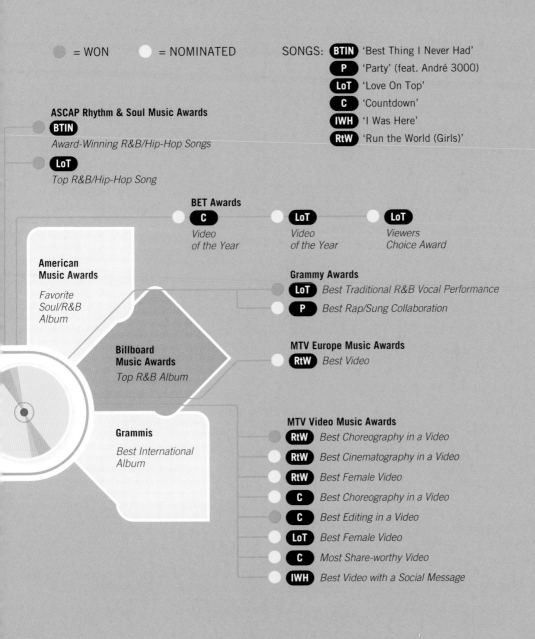

● = WON  ● = NOMINATED

SONGS: **BTIN** 'Best Thing I Never Had'
**P** 'Party' (feat. André 3000)
**LoT** 'Love On Top'
**C** 'Countdown'
**IWH** 'I Was Here'
**RtW** 'Run the World (Girls)'

**ASCAP Rhythm & Soul Music Awards**
**BTIN**
*Award-Winning R&B/Hip-Hop Songs*

**LoT**
*Top R&B/Hip-Hop Song*

**BET Awards**
**C** | **LoT** | **LoT**
*Video of the Year* | *Video of the Year* | *Viewers Choice Award*

**American Music Awards**
*Favorite Soul/R&B Album*

**Billboard Music Awards**
*Top R&B Album*

**Grammis**
*Best International Album*

**Grammy Awards**
**LoT** *Best Traditional R&B Vocal Performance*
**P** *Best Rap/Sung Collaboration*

**MTV Europe Music Awards**
**RtW** *Best Video*

**MTV Video Music Awards**
**RtW** *Best Choreography in a Video*
**RtW** *Best Cinematography in a Video*
**RtW** *Best Female Video*
**C** *Best Choreography in a Video*
**C** *Best Editing in a Video*
**LoT** *Best Female Video*
**C** *Most Share-worthy Video*
**IWH** *Best Video with a Social Message*

finished, than she was back in the global limelight, singing for the Obamas again. At their second Washington DC inauguration ceremony (following Barack's re-election), she sang the US anthem. There was a minor kerfuffle when newspapers revealed that she'd mimed to a pre-recorded tape. She had to hold a hastily convened press conference to defend her decision and her abilities. This she did with some style, asking the gathered journalists to stand up, and then belting out an impeccable – unquestionably live – rendition of 'The Star-Spangled Banner'. 'Any questions?' she asked, with true swagger.

She then gave a detailed explanation as to the necessity – on this occasion – of lip-syncing. 'I am a perfectionist … I practice until my feet bleed. I did not have time to rehearse with the orchestra. Due to no proper sound check, I did not feel comfortable taking a risk. It was about the president and the inauguration, and I wanted to make him and my country proud, so I decided to sing along with my pre-recorded track.' She insisted that this was 'common in the industry' and that she was proud of her performance.

Her next performance was arguably even bigger. That February's Super Bowl XLVII half-time show (she promised to sing live) proved to be the largest audience even she had faced. And she was ready. 'This is what I was born to do,' she enthused. 'I've had a sixteen-year career, and all the things I've done have prepared me for this.' Alicia Keys sang the anthem but the rest of the night's musical performance was all about Beyoncé.

Held at the Mercedes-Benz Superdome in New Orleans, her dazzling turn prompted a social media meltdown, with close to three hundred thousand tweets per minute documented. With 110.8 million TV viewers, it was the second most watched Super Bowl show ever, with only Madonna beating Beyoncé's record.

Apparently Jay-Z declined to cameo at the eleventh hour, deciding it was 'her moment' and he didn't want to 'take away from it'. Kelly Rowland and Michelle Williams did, however, guest, joining for a climactic run of 'Bootylicious' and 'Independent Women', and sticking around for 'Single Ladies'. Beyoncé opened with 'Run the World' and also crammed bits of 'Crazy in Love' and 'Halo' into a thrillingly busy twelve-minute set. That week, Beyoncé's digital download sales went up by eighty per cent, and those of Destiny's Child up by thirty-six per cent. The show – which involved an all-female band, an all-female horn section and the Saintsations, the host team's cheerleader troupe – received three Primetime Emmy nominations. She'd blown any sceptics away. 'She steered the half-time show away from dad rock to embrace girl power,' said the *Hollywood Reporter*. 'Why would you ever have a Super Bowl without Beyoncé?' asked *Rolling Stone*. 'Now that was a half-time show, and that was a star.'

Meanwhile she was still winning Grammys, with 'Love On Top' taking Best Traditional R&B Performance, even if her creative instincts were now shifting away from traditional R&B. An autobiographical documentary about the star, *Life Is But a Dream*, premiered on HBO on 16 February to nearly two million viewers, and was described by an awestruck (and weepy) Oprah Winfrey as 'a game-changer'. Many agreed that it showed that the superstar, who some nonbelievers sometimes complained came across as ruthlessly efficient, most definitely had a heart. It cleverly mixed live footage from the Atlantic City shows, slick promo material and personal laptop videos, to represent Beyoncé 'in her own words'. Indeed it did offer some vulnerability and candour, enriching a public image that, at this stage of fame and success, had been in danger of seeming remote. The narrative covered her marriage, her miscarriage, the birth of Blue Ivy and even her professional split with her father. Mathew didn't attend the New York premiere, though mother Tina, sister Solange, Kelly and Michelle did.

'I wouldn't have released a film just for the sake of self-documentation,' Beyoncé stated. 'I wanted it to express what I believe to be true about life – that it's not random, that everything has a reason, and that we need to be conscious of life's little clues and how the dots all connect, or we miss out.' Pressed by *GQ*, she revealed some of the big questions the documentary had prompted her to ponder:

How much do I reveal about myself? How do I keep my humility? How do I keep my spirit and the reality? How do I continue to be generous to my fans and to my craft? And how do I stay current? But how do I stay soulful? And this is the battle of my life. So when I walk onto a stage I'm able to come out of my shell and be as fabulous and over the top and strong and powerful as I want to be.

Of course, a superstar diva's notion of what's personal and frank isn't always the same as a journalist's or even a fan's. Comparisons were made to Madonna's *Truth or Dare*, and others deemed it contrived, but most concurred with *Billboard* that it was 'a pleasant surprise'. Taking it all in her stride, Beyoncé went back on the global road. April saw the opening of this new mum's epic next tour. Even its title got people talking. Some were surprised at the implied traditionalism in the name The Mrs. Carter Show World Tour. But 'Mrs. Carter,' she said, 'is who I am. More bold and fearless than I've ever been.'

**PREVIOUS PAGE:** Kelly Rowland, Beyoncé and Michelle Williams regroup as Destiny's Child at the Pepsi Super Bowl XLVII Halftime Show, 2013.
**RIGHT:** Beyoncé performs onstage during The Formation World Tour at the Rose Bowl in California, 2016.

# DRUNK IN LOVE

As her frenetic start to 2013 roundly demonstrated, anyone who thought motherhood might slow Beyoncé down was flat-out tripping. Now began her most ambitious and successful tour yet, easily that year's biggest by a solo artist, and indeed one of the decade's biggest by any artist. The Mrs. Carter Show World Tour opened in Belgrade, Serbia, on 15 April and ran through to the end of March the following year, closing in Lisbon, Portugal. Over seven legs and 132 gigs, the numbers were mind-boggling, with total gross takings of $230 million.

So it was a success. But that title seemed to many something of a betrayal of her constant advocacy of feminist 'independent woman' ideals. Her decision to be known as the wife of another celebrity rankled. 'Who runs the world? Husbands?' asked *Slate*. Her choice was described by the *Guardian* as 'subversive, but baffling'. It was posited in her defence that she had 'not only allowed her personal life to become more public but … has made family life her defining feature', and Jay-Z made frequent guest appearances throughout the tour. For fans and critics alike, the controversial decision raised questions for which there were no easy answers. Had Beyoncé substituted one male figure (her father) for another (Jay-Z)? Or was it in fact anti-feminist to criticize her choices and to prevent her from defining herself however she wanted to? Her confidence in assuming the role of 'Mrs. Carter', she told *Vogue*, 'comes from knowing my purpose and really knowing myself once I met my child. The purpose of my body became completely different.'

In any case, 'Mrs. Carter' wasn't the only persona on show. 'Queen Bey' was a presence, as the tour's visual and costume themes had her channelling various female monarchs (Marie Antoinette, Elizabeth I, Cleopatra) and employed designers from Givenchy to Julien Macdonald to Gucci. Tie-in clothes and perfume were marketed, and the only photographer allowed at her concerts was her personal lensman, Frank Micelotta. It confirmed that whatever people may

**RIGHT:** Blue Ivy Carter, Jay-Z and Beyoncé together at the 2014 MTV Video Music Awards, California.

# BEY'S *rider*

What does it take to keep Bey sweet backstage? Aside from a lot of protein and fruit, it doesn't take as much as you might think to keep her feeling Bootylicious when she's on the road.

## FOOD RIDER

Fresh-cut pineapple

Box of Special K with strawberries

Box of Great Grains Raisins, Nuts and Dates

Jar of Smuckers grape jelly

Jar of jalapeños and fresh jalapeños

Large turkey deli tray

## HOSPITALITY RIDER
### ALL WHITE FURNITURE

2 white rugs

White sofa

1.8 ft. table for catering with white tablecloth

White love seat

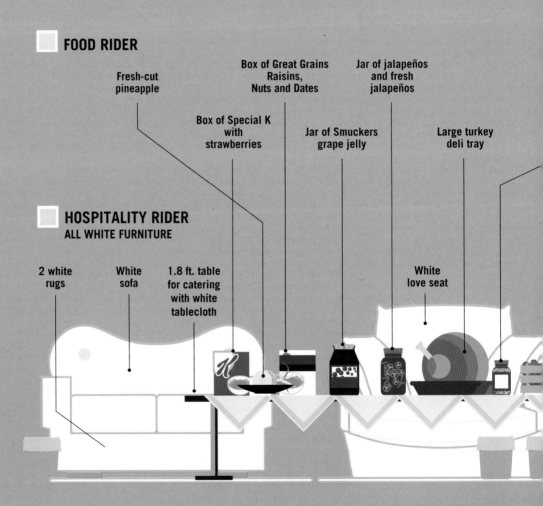

imagine of her various personas, the real woman behind the public image(s) was very much in control, and happy as a smart businessperson to actively exercise this control to attain the effects she desired as a creative artist. Also evident onstage were the Suga Mama band, films, fresh choreography, street dancers and a rope that transported a flying Beyoncé from the main stage to a second stage.

For her, the choreography was all about mixing up diverse styles to hit new heights and offer something to which differing cultures could all relate. She tapped into varying genres and modes, never afraid to seek the original within the time-honoured. As the novelist Zadie Smith wrote in October 2016,

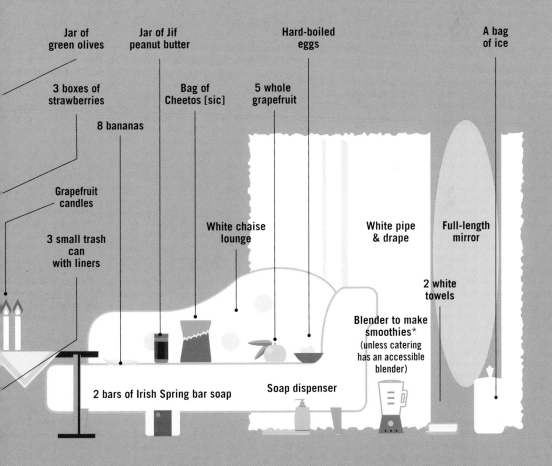

Jar of green olives

Jar of Jif peanut butter

Hard-boiled eggs

A bag of ice

3 boxes of strawberries

Bag of Cheetos [sic]

5 whole grapefruit

8 bananas

Grapefruit candles

White chaise lounge

White pipe & drape

Full-length mirror

3 small trash can with liners

2 white towels

Blender to make smoothies* (unless catering has an accessible blender)

2 bars of Irish Spring bar soap

Soap dispenser

'[Beyoncé] leads armies, and we join them. Beyoncé is … an apex. Here dancing is intended as a demonstration of the female will, a concrete articulation of its reach and possibilities.'

The exhilarating opening of the shows involved white-clad dancers marching across a stage-wide screen and crowning the regally attired Beyoncé. Through 'Run the World (Girls)' Beyoncé demonstrated female empowerment by showing aggression and authority, while the climax of 'Baby Boy' saw her offering some Dutty Wine (Jamaican dancehall-inspired) moves. During a medley of 'Naughty Girl' and 'Love to Love You Baby' she moved in front of an open fire display, the physical scenes suggesting burlesque stylings, while by contrast for 'Freakum Dress' two ballerinas accompanied her.

'I Miss You' witnessed Beyoncé singing in front of shadow dancers, and the tempo lifted for the Eighties neon lights and disco energy of 'Schoolin' Life'. By the time '1 + 1' began, the versatile diva was kneeling and then lying on top of the grand piano in a catsuit, while for 'Grown Woman' the African influences re-emerged in movement and costume, with the screen showing Beyoncé wearing a Nefertiti-era crown. As the tour moved on, new choreography was phased in, the constant perfectionist quest for improvement ongoing. ('Drunk in Love', when it arrived, was brought in with a reprise of a chair dance she'd premiered at the Grammy Awards.)

And while Beyoncé's efforts to get audiences to engage in a call-and-response of 'Hey, Mrs. Carter!' galled some of those who'd come to see Beyoncé rather than Jay-Z's other half, the audience was kept rapturously engaged by the rapid set changes, referencing everything from film noir to Las Vegas burlesque to fireworks to disco. As the predominant live spectacular extravaganza of its time, the show was variously compared to the heyday of Michael Jackson and Madonna and even to Cecil B. DeMille, and saw her labelled as 'the greatest entertainer of her generation'. Fans and critics alike revelled in her voice, her moves, her striking physical presence and her charisma. The *Independent*'s David Pollock opined that 'this two-hour epic is a ferocious distillation of musical styles old and new and a stunning declaration of intent that Knowles intends to be recognized as the defining pop artist of her era'.

**LEFT:** Beyoncé on stage in The Mrs. Carter Show World Tour, New York, 2013.

As ever, even on a tour this strenuous, Beyoncé kept other plates spinning. For Baz Luhrmann's film adaptation of *The Great Gatsby*, which would come out that same year, she'd contributed a cover of the late Amy Winehouse's 'Back to Black', working with André 3000. Jay-Z was executive producer on the soundtrack, as well as recording a track himself, and various artists from Lana Del Rey to Jack

# HIT ALBUM: *Beyoncé*

Beyoncé's self-titled album released in 2013 marked Queen Bey at peak creativity, with short films created for every single on the album. Reaching number one in the US Billboard charts immediately, its themes of sexuality, feminism and love delighted her fans and *Beyoncé* was met with critical acclaim the world over.

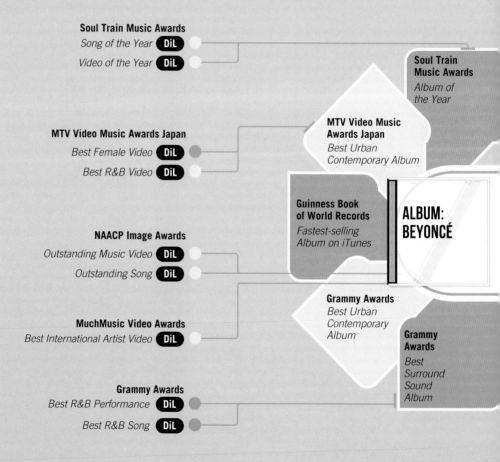

**Soul Train Music Awards**
*Song of the Year* **DiL**
*Video of the Year* **DiL**

**Soul Train Music Awards**
*Album of the Year*

**MTV Video Music Awards Japan**
*Best Female Video* **DiL**
*Best R&B Video* **DiL**

**MTV Video Music Awards Japan**
*Best Urban Contemporary Album*

**Guinness Book of World Records**
*Fastest-selling Album on iTunes*

**ALBUM: BEYONCÉ**

**NAACP Image Awards**
*Outstanding Music Video* **DiL**
*Outstanding Song* **DiL**

**Grammy Awards**
*Best Urban Contemporary Album*

**Grammy Awards**
*Best Surround Sound Album*

**MuchMusic Video Awards**
*Best International Artist Video* **DiL**

**Grammy Awards**
*Best R&B Performance* **DiL**
*Best R&B Song* **DiL**

White were involved. Queen Bey – or perhaps Mrs. Carter – also played the voice of Queen Tara, a kind of Mother Nature figure, in the colourful 3D CGI kids' movie *Epic*, and delivered a new song co-written with Sia, 'Rise Up', for it.

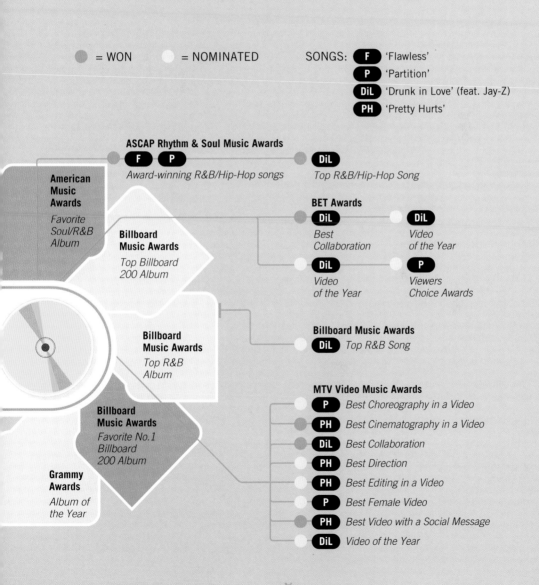

● = WON    ○ = NOMINATED    SONGS:    **F** 'Flawless'

**P** 'Partition'

**DiL** 'Drunk in Love' (feat. Jay-Z)

**PH** 'Pretty Hurts'

**ASCAP Rhythm & Soul Music Awards**

**F** **P**        **DiL**

*Award-winning R&B/Hip-Hop songs*    *Top R&B/Hip-Hop Song*

**American Music Awards**

*Favorite Soul/R&B Album*

**Billboard Music Awards**

*Top Billboard 200 Album*

**BET Awards**

**DiL**        **DiL**

*Best Collaboration*    *Video of the Year*

**DiL**        **P**

*Video of the Year*    *Viewers Choice Awards*

**Billboard Music Awards**

*Top R&B Album*

**Billboard Music Awards**    **DiL** *Top R&B Song*

**Billboard Music Awards**

*Favorite No.1 Billboard 200 Album*

**Grammy Awards**

*Album of the Year*

**MTV Video Music Awards**

**P** *Best Choreography in a Video*

**PH** *Best Cinematography in a Video*

**DiL** *Best Collaboration*

**PH** *Best Direction*

**PH** *Best Editing in a Video*

**P** *Best Female Video*

**PH** *Best Video with a Social Message*

**DiL** *Video of the Year*

A sensational year became an all-conquering one – Peak Beyoncé – with the surprise December release of her fifth album. Traditionally, big-league albums up until that point had been trailered and hyped to the point where the layman – never mind the ardent fan – couldn't fail to know they were imminent: in the music business, almost since day one, it's been a key part of building a buzz to trumpet a major release in advance and foster a frisson of anticipation. This, therefore, was a rule-shattering game-changer.

Titled just *Beyoncé*, and thus neatly precluding any Sasha-Fierce-was-more-feminist-than-Mrs.-Carter debates, it completely reinvented her persona yet again, with exceedingly timely grace. It placed her at the vanguard of contemporary popular culture with a heady mix of mystery, sex, experimentation and exquisite judgement. If her earlier eulogies for Jay-Z had grated with some, this was where her infatuation with her husband and sense of liberation paid dividends for loyal supporters. This new music truly was drunk in love: from the rhythms of 'Partition' to the sultry sexuality of 'Rocket', it was intoxicated and intoxicating, intimate and innovative. Her most unorthodox release was her tour de force.

Receiving almost as much attention as the tracks themselves was the way the album had been released. Of the shock-drop strategy, Beyoncé told *Billboard*,

## 'THERE'S SO MUCH THAT GETS BETWEEN THE MUSIC AND THE ART AND THE FANS.'

'I miss that immersive experience [of listening to albums], now that people only listen to a few seconds of a song on their iPods and don't really invest … it's all about the single, and the hype. There's so much that gets between the music and the art and the fans. I felt like … I just want this to come out when it's ready, and from me to my fans.'

It was ready, for sure. Developed as an audio-visual entity with a parallel accompaniment of short films, *Beyoncé* was broodier and deeper than anything she'd put out previously. Revelling in complete creative freedom, *Beyoncé* addresses love, sex and other relationship issues with a genuine, explicit, almost unsettling artistic candour. It was also her most sonically inventive record, embracing the cutting edge of current popular music.

The making of this marvel began in secret, when Beyoncé invited a select number of writers and producers to live alongside her and Jay-Z in the Hamptons,

New York, for a month in summer 2012. These were big names, too: Justin Timberlake, Timbaland, Sia and The-Dream were among the guests. It was a productive atmosphere, yet relaxed and convivial too. 'We had dinner every day with the producers, like a family,' she told *Vogue*. 'It was like a camp … weekends off. You could go and jump in the pool and ride bikes. The ocean, the grass, the sunshine … it really was a safe place.' She divided her days between tending to her new baby and spending time in the studio. Sia's 'Pretty Hurts', which came to open the album, was conceived here. More recording took place in two New York City studios – Jungle City and Oven – in 2013.

There was then a pause as she toured. But even in transit, she tweaked her concepts, bringing in then-little-known electronica producer Boots, who was to be the album's break-out hero. He'd fronted rock bands such as Blonds, and Jay-Z had snapped him up to Roc Nation on a publishing deal. He didn't meet Beyoncé till June 2013, and was surprised to find she was keener on the more unconventional material he'd held back. Some of his trance-based hypnotic work spoke to her; by his account, she would pick up on snippets and spy an unforeseen potential in them. 'The only visionary in the room,' he called her, and said visionary elected to use him on three quarters of the album.

Inspired, she began dropping in archive footage from her life story, from her childhood 'defeat' on TV show *Star Search* to feminist speeches and recollections of the early girl-group days. Even a sinus infection didn't stop her, as she decided it only helped her vocal on 'XO'. The clinchers for the album, however, were moments of pure spontaneous inspiration. She and Jay-Z put their vocals and rap together for 'Drunk in Love' over a beat provided by Timbaland and Detail, with a high level of freestyling (and much eroticized flirting). 'Partition', equally, if not more suggestive, was so raunchy that at first she drew back, embarrassed. Happily for her listeners, she would overcome her reservations and carry on with the track, unabashed. For the opening section of another track, 'Yoncé', the beat was begun by Justin Timberlake, rather less erotically, hitting buckets. With this album, it seemed, she'd nurtured an openly creative atmosphere and there was nothing she and her allies were afraid to try.

During Thanksgiving week the call went out to all the confidential collaborators to get mixes completed, and Beyoncé adopted a refreshingly instant-decision, snap-verdict, gut-feeling approach to the editing of her vocals.

She'd always known she wanted to make this a surprise 'overnight' release: now that fantasy was to become real. She was 'bored' with predictable, bog-standard marketing. The code name 'Lily' was used in top-secret meetings with Columbia and iTunes; the record company head cunningly misdirected the media by telling them a new album from the star would be out in 2014. And then, *Beyoncé* was suddenly out there, taking people's breath away. A week after its iTunes release, physical copies were distributed on 20 December, just in time for Christmas. On 21 December all the attendant videos were screened at New York's SVA Theatre.

The internet, of course, exploded. Fans veered on hysteria. The tactic probably gained more publicity than any conventional marketing drive could have done. In a multi-choice, fragmented pop culture, we were all – unusually – listening to the same thing at the same time. 'A bombshell,' said *Rolling Stone*'s Rob Sheffield.

> Beyoncé has delivered countless surprises in her fifteen years on top of the music world, but never like this. Queen Bey woke the world in the midnight hour with a 'visual album' – fourteen new songs, seventeen videos, dropped via iTunes with no warning. The whole project is a celebration of the Beyoncé philosophy, which basically boils down to … Beyoncé can do anything the hell she wants to.

The *Guardian*'s Peter Robinson coined the phrase 'Beyoncégeddon', hailing it as a major triumph and 'a masterclass in both exerting and relinquishing control'. Soon other artists were following the strategy, from Drake to Radiohead. A year on, Harvard Business School was studying the release as a nonpareil of planning and execution: a highly credible sign that Beyoncé was now simultaneously hitting the zenith of her creative inspiration and the peak of her business and marketing acumen.

While traditional promotion had been cleverly circumnavigated, allowing a titillated Twitter to do the heavy lifting, Beyoncé – still on tour when the album dropped – did embrace some more conventional marketing, incorporating tracks from the new album into her set list from that point. In January 2014 she gave her debut performance of 'Drunk in Love' at the Grammy Awards (with the

**RIGHT:** Beyoncé performs 'Drunk in Love' on stage at the 56th Grammy Awards in LA, 2014.

aforementioned chair dance), while its video – a black-and-white classic directed by Hype Williams, showing Mr and Mrs Carter getting steamy on a Florida beach – caused further buzz.

'Drunk in Love' is arguably an artist-redefining album's defining moment. Rarely before had Beyoncé, long respected for her superhuman abilities, sounded so touchingly human, so emotional yet cool, so intimate and charged. Her sensual, confident, teasing vocal lilted over trap beats and fully backed up the singer's view that she'd 'had a party, just had fun' recording it. The lyrics expressed how much she enjoyed making love with her partner, using a series of double entendres and reshaping the meaning of the word 'surfboard' for a generation of women, whilst Jay-Z's rap is even more explicit, painting a highly eroticized portrait of desire. Despite the danger of his swagger tactics spoiling the effect of Beyoncé's more subtle grace and guile, the steamy number got the green light from newcomers as well as long-time devotees. The fluid, chorus-spurning duet, spiritually the heir to Madonna's 'Justify My Love', was a kind of R-rated sequel to 'Crazy in Love', and stands with it as Beyoncé's recording career zenith. (Some would argue that 'Single Ladies' ranks up there as their rival.) It was far better than any record where a married couple get jiggy has a reasonable right to be. It somehow pulled off the magic trick of being completely filthy and yet warmly romantic.

The album, which showed how much the new Queen Bey had evolved from the slightly prim mainstream entertainer of yore, was her most acclaimed yet. Its overt feminist themes (insecurity, bulimia and postnatal depression were touched on), unapologetically ecstatic sexuality and loose, contemporary, gritty sounds were deliciously dense and humid. In eschewing any attempt to chase a safe market, it gained her limitless respect.

Even though it had been released so late in the year, it swept up many critics' album-of-the-year polls, including *Billboard*, the *Los Angeles Times* and – proving she was still adored in her old hometown – the *Houston Chronicle*. (By 2015, *Billboard* was elevating it to the best album of the decade so far.) For others it ranked alongside Michael Jackson's *Thriller* as not just a great pop album, but as a grand statement and momentous event. Calling Beyoncé 'the greatest female R&B artist of the century' *GQ* rejoiced that she'd 'finally made a record as sexy, snarling, soft, strange, and outright superlative as she is'. *Pitchfork* confessed that they'd imagined the 'seasoned pro' moving towards 'blandness' at this stage in her career, but instead she'd actually become more adventurous and was expressing 'an alternate vision of adulthood'. The bottom line was that *Beyoncé* was so good that its strengths and personality became its defining characteristics, overshadowing even its maverick manner of release.

As if this wasn't enough, it made her the first woman in history to have her first five (studio) albums go straight in at number one. One million copies were sold digitally even before the physical release a week later. Nearly half a million in the first twenty-four hours. These were the highest first-week figures of even her career. It was also the fastest mover in the history of the iTunes store to date and has been certified double platinum. It's safe to say motherhood was suiting her.

The Carters were still so giddy on love that, in April 2014, they announced their first co-headlining stadium tour. As The Mrs. Carter Show World Tour and Jay-Z's Magna Carter World Tour had both reached their end, the pair embarked on the On the Run Tour, its name taken from a Jay-Z track on which his wife had guested. The poster for the shows played on their 'rebel/outlaw' Bonnie and Clyde image, showing them hugging while wearing balaclavas, only her iconic eyes instantly recognizable. There was also a movie-style trailer, showing them in bloody R-rated action sequences, guns blazing. Celebs making cameos included Jake Gyllenhaal, Don Cheadle, Sean Penn, Rashida Jones, Blake Lively and Emmy Rossum. Videos echoing this played during the shows themselves, Beyoncé happily embracing her 'bad girl' side.

The tour ran from late June through to mid-September, with nineteen dates in America then just two in Europe (in the couple's beloved Paris). It still grossed over $100 million and was the fifth biggest of the year. HBO screened a composite of their two French concerts (where Nicki Minaj guested). The set list on the tour kept the Carters switching over throughout the night, taking turns as it were, and the pair won praise for balancing their time in the spotlight. 'The coordination is not just remarkable,' wrote *USA Today*, 'it's the absolute best way that two of the world's best performers can deliver a show that proves why they're on top together.'

**NEXT PAGE:** Jay-Z and Beyoncé perform together on their On the Run Tour, Pasadena 2014.

# COUNT*down*

The graphic below shows the top five female artists who have recorded five or more Billboard number one studio albums (compilation albums and live recordings are excluded here). Impressive percentages are shown for how many of those albums reached number one for each artist, but Queen Bey stands out as the only star to hit the top spot with every one of her albums.

## THE TOP 5

| | | |
|---|---|---|
| **Beyoncé:** | 6 out of 6 albums | ●●●●●● |
| **Britney Spears:** | 6 out of 8 albums | ●●●●●●●○ |
| **Madonna:** | 8 out of 13 albums | ●●●●●●●●○○○○○ |
| **Janet Jackson:** | 6 out of 10 albums | ●●●●●●○○○○ |
| **Mariah Carey:** | 6 out of 13 albums | ●●●●●●○○○○○○○ |

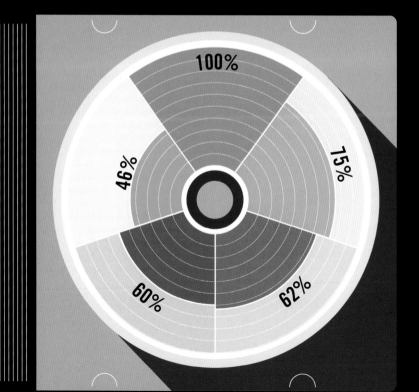

Jay-Z had murmured to the BBC the previous year that a joint tour was 'slowly making more sense, more sense every day', and his regular appearances during her solo shows had made it almost an inevitability. Ultimately it was planned and put together quickly – relatively, for such a huge undertaking. The pair had evidently brainstormed on what messages the show might convey. As ever, they were determined to do things their way, to not just trot through industry-standard motions. The *Miami Times* reported the themes of On the Run as displaying the pair being on the run from 'the media, their place in pop music, the haters, the bullshit, and sometimes even each other'. They didn't elaborate on the last part, but it was just another example of their newfound candour. Jay-Z tried to clarify the concept, speaking to MTV. 'We're not trying to do this literally,' he laughed. 'It's not that we're Bonnie and Clyde. We're on the run from everything. On the run from being a cliché. On the run from doing the same thing again.' As Beyoncé's album had proved, she was now flush with creativity, resistant to tired repetition and bursting with energetic originality.

Versace was one of her designers for the touring wardrobe, and she wore a bedazzled black leather bodysuit, another more colourful one, which Versace described as having a 'baseball vibe', and a bridal veil and train (16 feet long) made from a monochrome American flag. The last outfit took over 500 hours to make. America's alternative sweetheart was still challenging convention. Alexander Wang contributed a 'bondage' body-suit, while Diesel offered a shorts-and-jacket outfit inspired by Texas biker gangs. Diesel's designer Nicola Formichetti called the look 'one part police officer and two parts jailbait'.

If the last phrase was wilfully controversial, Beyoncé's choices with the subversion of traditionalized female entertainer roles were knowing and deliberate. She was always adamant that gender equality and women's rights were high on her agenda. In a tricky, often confused time for mainstream culture, Beyoncé's representations of 'woman' rarely kowtowed to the male gaze, aware that much progress had been made in the Nineties by indie-rock's Riot Grrrl movement, and by the likes of P.J. Harvey, Björk, Tori Amos and others since. Her work now harmonized with third wave feminism's 'freedom of choice' philosophy, whereby sexual objectification could be conscientiously chosen, or used, by an artist as a device to exhibit confidence and assertiveness. Such messages showed younger girls that the terms and codes of female sexuality were theirs to control.

As Madonna had embraced her own sexuality in an earlier era, now Beyoncé was proving that how she dressed or moved was not decreed by any patriarchal group, but by herself. If males were having fantasies about the pop figure they perceived, the messages, aimed at women, were going over their heads. Here, liberty was actively seized by the artist, not granted to a passive female puppet by males.

# THE COST OF LOOKING
## *a million dollars*

Beyoncé might say she 'woke up like that', but the rumour-mill says otherwise. Here are a few of the whispered costs of looking a million dollars.

- **Hair and makeup.** Her hair extensions for The Mrs. Carter Show World Tour alone are said to have cost $145,000.

- **One pair of shoes.** In 2015, Bey is said to have spent this on a pair of House of Borgezie Princess Constellation stilettos covered in 1,290 precious stones.

- **A personal trainer** and other fitness-related costs.

- Twice-weekly meetings with a **nutritionist**.

- **On mani- and pedicures.** She's said to pay out $85 per nail when she has a gold manicure.

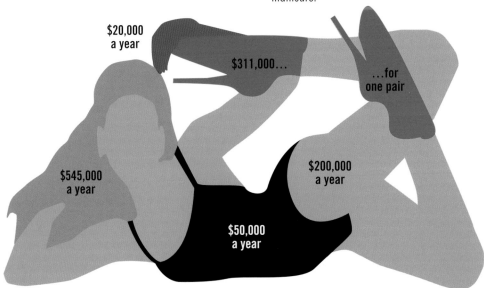

$20,000 a year

$311,000...

...for one pair

$545,000 a year

$200,000 a year

$50,000 a year

Beyoncé herself had written, in a January 2014 piece for *The Shriver Report*, that 'equality will be achieved when men and women are granted equal pay and equal respect', and in a *Vogue* interview she turned questioner, asking, 'Why do you have to choose what type of woman you are? Why do you have to label yourself anything? I'm just a woman and I love being a woman.' Asked about the sensuous grinding that was part of her performance in many shows and videos, she responded, 'I was very aware of the fact that I was showing my body. I wanted to show that you can have a child, and you can work hard, and you can get your body back.' Like all the best artists, she defied simplistic definition.

She was also against the sexual stereotyping of women. President Obama's quote that she 'could not be a better role model for my girls' was dragged out and attacked after the highly sensual *Beyoncé* album, but her defenders questioned why she could not be, at the same time, sexual and 'respectable'. With many parts of the media still taking an ultraconservative approach to female sexuality, Beyoncé deliberately trod a fine line, highlighting the conflicting demands of a society that

## 'I'M JUST A WOMAN AND I LOVE BEING A WOMAN.'

wants women to be sexy, but not *too* sexy. And she wasn't afraid to stand her ground. 'I feel like I've earned the right to be me and to express any and every side of myself,' she stated.

Her 'Pretty Hurts' video had emphasized how all women in the music industry were constantly under pressure to sell sexual desirability, but at the same time portrayed her as taking part in a beauty contest. In the very contradictions, in the paradox, lay the heart of the inquisitive creative Beyoncé: wise to the fact that she must appear 'ordinary' but at the same time, as a celebrity, 'extraordinary'. As she sang on the track 'Grown Woman': 'I'm a grown woman, I can do whatever I want.' She called the shots, and inspired others to embrace their sexual identity, and own it.

Pausing only to collect the Video Vanguard Award at the 2014 MTV Video Music Awards (as well as two gongs for the 'Pretty Hurts' video and one for 'Drunk in Love'), Beyoncé reissued the latest album in extended editions in November 2014. And she was not just being recognized for her creativity and inventiveness, her business acuity and entrepreneurialism were paying off, too. She was listed by *Forbes* as the highest-earning female in music – for the second consecutive year. In a single year she'd more than doubled 2013's takings, bringing home a staggering $115 million. According to *Billboard*, she was now the highest earning black artist over one year of all time, overtaking the previous records of Michael Jackson, Janet Jackson and Prince.

Of course not all this workaholic's wealth had come from lucrative touring and radical recording. She'd long since become a face everybody wanted on their adverts. She'd been smart and selective as a businesswoman, whenever possible only associating with choice brands, but shrewd enough to know when a high street link-up would promote her tastefully. Pepsi had been the chief starting point. She'd signed with them in 2002 and, two years later, had appeared in a commercial alongside Britney Spears, Pink and Enrique Iglesias. By 2012, her stature had grown to such an extent that Pepsi were prepared to offer her a staggering $50 million deal to continue to endorse the soft drink, a great deal more than her original fee a decade earlier – and one she accepted.

Fashion was always one of her great loves, as had been showcased by her early-career collaborations with her mother, Tina, on costumes and stage outfits. She'd then graduated to working with Tommy Hilfiger on the fragrances True Star and True Star Gold. (For these she'd sung a cover of Rose Royce's wistful, gossamer-light ballad 'Wishing on a Star'.) In 2010, more significantly, she launched her own fragrance, named Heat. For the commercial she appeared seemingly unclad, crooning the steamy 'Fever'. The temperature was kept high for the fragrance's 'sequel', Heat Rush, and within a year she'd launched a third, Pulse. Various limited edition fragrances followed, tying in with tours, and at the last count the six editions of Heat have amassed startling sales of over $400 million. This being Beyoncé, that's the best-selling celebrity fragrance line of all.

There have been occasional hiccups within her extra-curricular ventures: a video game (*Starpower: Beyoncé*) was cancelled when she withdrew from the project, and an out-of-court settlement was reached. Yet her list of successful sponsorship deals is textbook, from American Express to Nintendo DS. And let's not forget she'd begun her enduring relationship with L'Oréal at age eighteen. From around the same age, she'd cited her own fashion heroes as Tina Turner ('she made her strength feminine and sexy') and Marilyn Monroe ('because she was a curvy woman: I'm drawn to things that have the same kind of silhouettes as what she wore, because our bodies are similar').

In 2014 there was a partnering-up with Britain's Topshop clothes retailer, to launch an 'active wear' label for 'clothing, footwear, and accessories across dance, fitness and sports categories'. A practised diplomat, Beyoncé said, 'I have always loved Topshop for its forward thinking.' Her own forward thinking was soon to outgrow such deals and aim even higher.

As with all the other strings to her bow, she'd put the hard yards in. In 2005, she'd launched a fashion line with her stylist mother, House of Deréon (named in honour of her seamstress grandmother), as well as Beyond Productions, which looked after the brand's licensing and brand management. 'The whole thing is taking nothing and turning it into something, because that's what my grandmother did with all kinds of fabrics,' said Beyoncé. Adding that her grandmother and mother turned everything into masterpieces, she unwittingly begged a generational comparison: she had proven no slouch at alchemy herself. House of Deréon coined the slogan: 'Where the sidewalk and the catwalk meet.' Cleverly reaching out to the audiences of Oprah Winfrey and Tyra Banks by targeting their TV shows, and with sister Solange onboard, they'd expanded into shoes and footwear, and a mobile game, featuring the Deréon collection, called *Beyoncé Fashion Diva*. When Beyoncé and Solange are modelling your clothes on your posters, you're in business. By

**'THE WHOLE THING IS TAKING NOTHING AND TURNING IT INTO SOMETHING.'**

2009 the Sasha Fierce for Deréon junior and back-to-school line was active, and distributed through Macy's and other huge chains. The following year C&A launched Deréon by Beyoncé across Brazil, as she 'cross-platformed' into conquering a fresh continent. It seemed that since marrying Jay-Z, new and bold ideas were springing up – not least a clothing line part-named after their daughter – and about to swell into a tidal wave …

For the diversely triumphant diva, 2015 was scarcely less exhilarating than her *annus mirabilis*, and got off to an auspicious start as she continued her tradition of bossing the Grammys. This time she won three: 'Drunk in Love' garnering Best R&B Song and Best R&B Performance, while the album took

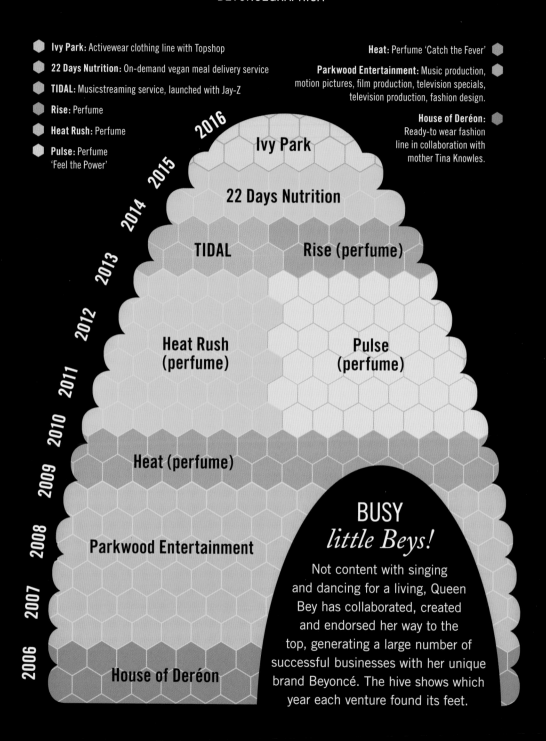

**Ivy Park:** Activewear clothing line with Topshop

**22 Days Nutrition:** On-demand vegan meal delivery service

**TIDAL:** Musicstreaming service, launched with Jay-Z

**Rise:** Perfume

**Heat Rush:** Perfume

**Pulse:** Perfume 'Feel the Power'

**Heat:** Perfume 'Catch the Fever'

**Parkwood Entertainment:** Music production, motion pictures, film production, television specials, television production, fashion design.

**House of Deréon:** Ready-to wear fashion line in collaboration with mother Tina Knowles.

2016

**Ivy Park**

2015

**22 Days Nutrition**

2014

**TIDAL**

**Rise (perfume)**

2013

2012

**Heat Rush (perfume)**

**Pulse (perfume)**

2011

2010

2009

**Heat (perfume)**

2008

**Parkwood Entertainment**

2007

2006

**House of Deréon**

## BUSY
*little Beys!*

Not content with singing and dancing for a living, Queen Bey has collaborated, created and endorsed her way to the top, generating a large number of successful businesses with her unique brand Beyoncé. The hive shows which year each venture found its feet.

Best Surround Sound Album. To the surprise of most, she was pipped to Album of the Year by Beck's *Morning Phase*.

Yet Beyoncé enjoyed cultural cache of a level Beck could never know. She was in a league of her own. The *New Yorker* described her as 'the most important and compelling popular musician of the twenty-first century. The result, the logical end point, of a century-plus of pop.' She was the *Guardian*'s Artist of the Decade: 'She and not any superannuated rock star was the greatest live performer of the past ten years.' And when she ruled the *Time* 100 list, flamboyant film director Baz Luhrmann wrote a eulogy, claiming that nobody could match her for 'that voice … the way she moves … no one can hold an audience the way she does. When Beyoncé does an album, sings a song, does anything – it's an event, and it's broadly influential. Right now, she is the heir apparent diva of the USA – the reigning national voice.'

Yet if it seemed as if Beyoncé couldn't possibly top her own catalogue of achievements, well, she could. She was about to take what life would give her and make a distinctly fresh lemonade …

# MAKING LEMONADE

As the most powerful female in entertainment, according to *Forbes'* 2015 Power List, Queen Bey could do no wrong. She could even relax at the 2016 Grammys, with no pressure on her to prove anything, as Kendrick Lamar and Taylor Swift duked it out for the main gongs, and Lady Gaga and Nile Rodgers strived to pay tribute to the newly departed genius David Bowie. (By August, a rejuvenated Beyoncé would be mastering those awards ceremonies again …)

Alongside the musical achievements of the previous year, she was also now a co-owner of Tidal, the subscription-based music streaming service that Jay-Z had launched at a high-profile press conference in spring 2015. Supported by Madonna, Rihanna, Chris Martin, Kanye West, Alicia Keys, Jack White and other A-list friends and allies from varied musical genres, Jay-Z embarked on a much-discussed mass-marketing campaign. 'Tidal For All', ran the hashtag. It was pitched as the first 'artist-owned' streaming service, and as having 'a vision to change the status quo'. While it probably hasn't swept the world to the extent that Jay-Z and gang hoped, Tidal has, at the time of writing, reached over thirty countries and has over four million paying subscribers.

If Beyoncé was content to pass on performing at this year's Grammy Awards, she was not about to let the Super Bowl 50 half time show go by without making a resonant impact. And it wasn't, strictly, even her gig. The show, at Levi's Stadium, Santa Clara, California, celebrated the Super Bowl's half-century, with Coldplay headlining and Bruno Mars and Mark Ronson guesting. But it was Mrs Carter who stole the headlines. Coldplay performed tracks old and new either side of Mars and Ronson delivering some 'Uptown Funk', and then Beyoncé made everyone forget everything else with a show incorporating a political statement that transcended – and reinvigorated the force of – popular culture. When she fired out new song 'Formation', she prompted awe and provoked controversy. She'd released the track and its video the night before, exclusively on Tidal as free downloads. On 7 February, she took things to the next level.

Black Lives Matter (BLM) as an international activist movement had begun in the States in 2013 after the acquittal of George Zimmerman in the shooting of African-American teenager Trayvon Martin. Its street demonstrations raised its profile after the controversial deaths of further African-Americans. The debates around the issues were and remain highly sensitive and heated. For Beyoncé – or any popular artist – to get involved was the polar opposite of a cosy career move. Her statement on this huge occasion therefore was all the more striking. She arguably hadn't previously been perceived as the most ardent of activists but this bold stand against inequality revealed that she was becoming more of an agitator for social justice than perhaps anybody had perceived.

Entering in a black leather Michael Jackson-inspired outfit, accompanied by backing dancers dressed in Seventies' Black Panther berets, her team's mass

> '...TO RAISE SOCIAL CONSCIOUSNESS AND USE THEIR ARTISTRY TO ADVANCE SOCIAL JUSTICE.'
>
> **MELINA ABDULLAH, BLACK LIVES MATTER**

choreography stunned audiences only slightly less than the striking sociological statement of a Black Power salute. She then joined in on an extra refrain of 'Uptown Funk' and sang with pal Chris Martin's band. But all anyone was talking about the next day was her pugilistic 'Formation', which included graffiti reading 'Stop Shooting Us' and the dancers forming an X to signify Malcolm X. Coldplay might as well have been a warm-up act. On the day, 115 million people watched. And while many were wowed, some were angry.

Black Lives Matter activist Melina Abdullah praised her and other artists who were 'willing to raise social consciousness and use their artistry to advance social justice'. Beyoncé's courage in doing so was confirmed as some prominent conservatives criticized what they perceived as an 'anti-police' message in her performance, and former New York City mayor Rudy Giuliani accused her of playing with fire by using Black Power symbolism at a delicate moment. (It was

**NEXT PAGE:** Beyoncé performs 'Formation' at The Super Bowl 50 Halftime Show in California, 2016.

# GLOBAL *profit*

Queen Bey's touring schedule is phenomenal and the graph below shows which of her mesmerizing global tours has attracted the most fans and generated the most profit in dollars.

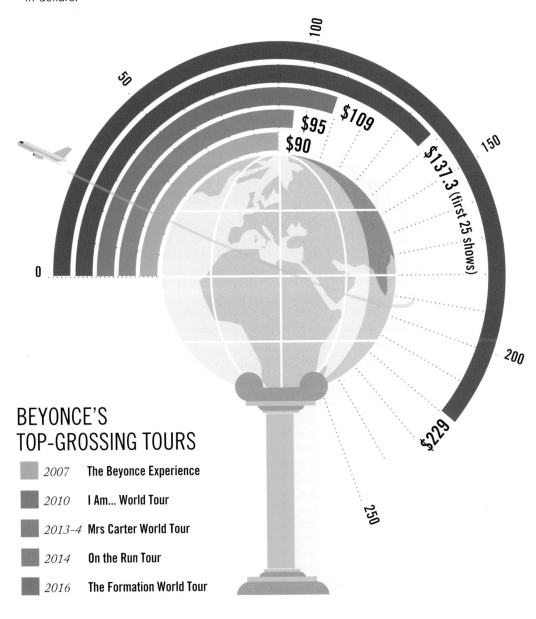

100

50

$95

$109

$90

$137.3 (first 25 shows)

150

0

200

$229

250

## BEYONCE'S TOP-GROSSING TOURS

| | | |
|---|---|---|
| | *2007* | **The Beyonce Experience** |
| | *2010* | **I Am... World Tour** |
| | *2013-4* | **Mrs Carter World Tour** |
| | *2014* | **On the Run Tour** |
| | *2016* | **The Formation World Tour** |

also the fiftieth anniversary of the Black Panther Party.) A #boycottBeyoncé hashtag even briefly flickered up on Twitter, and an anti-Beyoncé rally was mooted … but, tellingly, nobody showed up.

CNN hit back by calling some of the criticisms of Beyoncé 'racially motivated'. She'd certainly got her point out there: it had been the third-highest watched show in history in the States.

If Rudy didn't want to join the BeyHive fan army (including seventy-seven million followers on Instagram alone), many did. The lyrics of 'Formation' were also outspoken on the matters of race and skin colour (as well as some lyrical revelations about her married sex life), but still found time for Beyoncé to state that she 'came to slay, bitch', instantly laying claim to a new catchphrase. Mother Tina 'slayed', too, posting a photograph of herself and the dancers giving a Black Power one-fist salute after the show. Beyoncé wasn't just paying lip service either: she posted messages about police shootings of black people and wrote on her website – in black lettering on a white screen – 'We are sick and tired of the killings of young men and women in our communities. It is up to us to take a stand and demand that they "stop killing us".' She was a target for flak when police officers were shot soon afterwards, but was unapologetic, and unequivocal in stating, 'No violence will create peace. To effect change we must show love in the face of hate and peace in the face of violence.' Nobody could deny her commitment.

Her courage to address such divisive, incendiary issues might have derailed the career of a less established superstar, but she'd won so much respect that people listened. She did it through art as well as articulation: the 'Formation' video showed a young black child dancing in front of a line of riot police, and Beyoncé atop a New Orleans police car sinking into water, referencing the tragedies of 2005's Hurricane Katrina. Beyoncé had been involved in fundraising after the hurricane, which killed 1,200 people along the Gulf Coast. The government had been criticized for a response that was widely perceived as inadequate, particularly in poorer communities or those that were largely African-American. Now, debate around 'Formation' continued heatedly. The National Sheriffs' director argued, with what you might call a loose grip on calm judgement, 'It's inciting bad behaviour. Art is one thing, but shouting fire in a crowded theatre is an entirely different one.' Beyoncé retorted that she wasn't irresponsibly sending out anti-police signals. She told *Elle*, 'I have so much admiration and respect for officers and their families, who sacrifice themselves to keep us safe. But let's be clear: I am against police brutality and injustice. Those are two separate things.' She put her money where her mouth was, raising $1.5 million for Black Lives Matter groups with a Tidal tie-in concert.

She kept up the momentum as she took to the road again. Straight after the controversial Super Bowl show she announced The Formation World Tour, her seventh, was to visit America and Europe across 2016. Her website crashed after tickets went on sale. It ran from a Miami show on 27 April to Nashville on 2 October, over four legs, and had passed the $200-million gross mark by late summer. It was, of course, another sensory-overload spectacular, featuring a 60 foot-high rotating LED box – named The Monolith – as well as a runway and a second stage area with startling cascading water features that left Beyoncé, at the show's climax, eye-catchingly splashing and drenched. It was described as 'a game-changer for what can be achieved in a stadium touring environment' and 'an epic experience'. The credit went to Es Devlin, designer, and engineering/ building companies Stageco and Tait Towers. Devlin said of the LED box that she wanted it to be 'the tallest object in the stadium, a piece of kinetic stadium architecture the equivalent of a seven-storey, revolving LED building … an armour within which Beyoncé is revealed as an all-too-human-scale, real-life figure'. She stressed that that real-life figure was at every stage involved in the complex creative process.

The costumes, naturally, 'slayed', with Beyoncé styled by Marni Senofonte in outfits referencing Africa, the Wild West, 'the antebellum South' and even sadomasochism. For her hometown appearance in Houston, her bodysuit was embellished with a black-beaded panther. While it wasn't stated explicitly, it's easy to read that as another political point-score. In London, at Wembley, she debuted a gold leotard, designed by British icon Julien Macdonald, adorned with seventy thousand Swarovski crystals. Crowds left the shows giddy with her force and finesse, energy and electricity, and demonstrations of modern girl power. Critics acknowledged that she was 'this generation's Michael Jackson' and that 'when it comes to sheer innovation, showmanship and creativity, Beyoncé has

# COSTUME *drama*

Beyoncé's onstage outfits slay and each sartorial choice carefully reflects the themes and attitude of her tours. It seems that as Queen Bey's star shines brighter, so do her costumes for each tour, in style and in number.

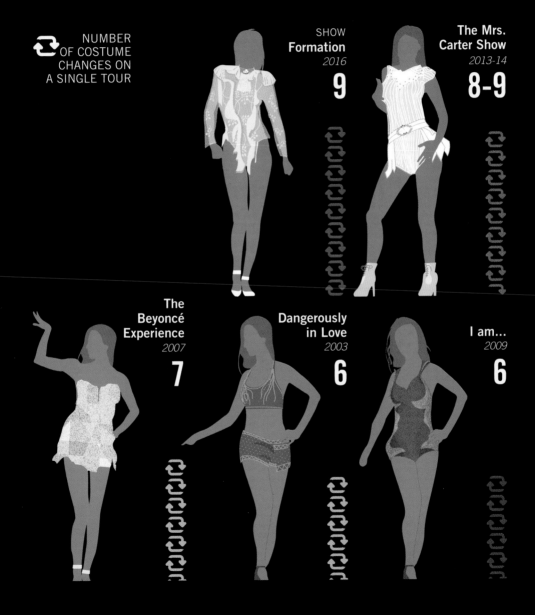

NUMBER OF COSTUME CHANGES ON A SINGLE TOUR

SHOW
**Formation**
*2016*

**9**

**The Mrs. Carter Show**
*2013-14*

**8-9**

**The Beyoncé Experience**
*2007*

**7**

**Dangerously in Love**
*2003*

**6**

**I am...**
*2009*

**6**

everyone else beaten'. Others swooned that 'She sounds, moves and looks like a goddess, and most of us bow down accordingly.'

The concert opened explosively, with 'Formation', the song she'd debuted at the Super Bowl. By now the album it had so effectively teased had burst out. Before the tour began, on 16 April, she'd released a tantalizing trailer for *Lemonade*, which, it was revealed, was an hour-long movie, premiered on HBO a week later. The same day, Tidal exclusively released the sibling album of the same name. Beyoncé promptly became the first act ever to debut atop the Billboard chart with her first six studio albums.

Incredibly, *Lemonade* won even greater acclaim than any of her previous releases. It reiterated that the singer was not about to retreat into any comfort zone. Perhaps even more politically aware than 'Formation' was 'Freedom', an empowerment anthem for black women. Its lyrics covered historical slavery of African-Americans and contemporary police brutality and racial profiling. (The video poignantly showed the mothers of

## 'A SURPRISINGLY FURIOUS SONG-CYCLE ABOUT INFIDELITY AND REVENGE.'

### WASHINGTON POST

Trayvon Martin, Michael Brown and Eric Garner, all killed by the police, with the women holding up pictures of their lost sons.) Beyoncé performed the song a cappella in some shows. She was taking her role as one of the most prominent champions of the Black Lives Matter movement with due seriousness. In a way this was a natural and bold evolution from her calls for female independence and solidarity in her younger Destiny's Child days, but her impassioned commitment – and her willingness to stare down any right-wing backlash – was truly inspirational for many.

Yet *Lemonade* was also inspiring in its musical eclecticism and imaginative effervescence. If its spine was R&B, it refused to accept genre boundaries or even time periods, racing across hip-hop, rock, pop, soul and funk, gospel, trap and even a dash of country. The catholic list of star guests confirmed this, from rock guitarist Jack White to current hip-hop king Kendrick Lamar, from British post-dubstep experimentalist James Blake to Canadian alternative R&B act The Weeknd. It sampled everyone from Isaac Hayes to Led Zeppelin to Andy Williams: a broad church. Solidly placing Beyoncé now as a challenging albums

# MAKING *Lemonade*

Beyoncé's album *Lemonade* draws from multiple musical genres and many of the songs on the album are recognizably influenced by a particular style of music.

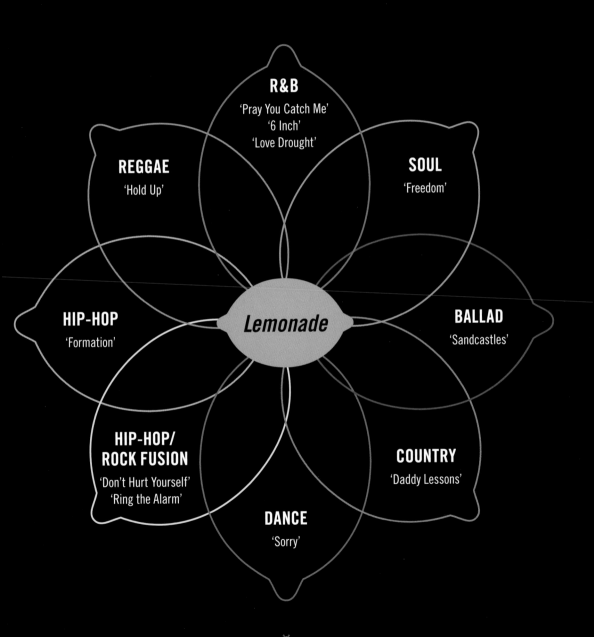

**R&B**
'Pray You Catch Me'
'6 Inch'
'Love Drought'

**REGGAE**
'Hold Up'

**SOUL**
'Freedom'

**HIP-HOP**
'Formation'

*Lemonade*

**BALLAD**
'Sandcastles'

**HIP-HOP/
ROCK FUSION**
'Don't Hurt Yourself'
'Ring the Alarm'

**COUNTRY**
'Daddy Lessons'

**DANCE**
'Sorry'

# THAT'S WHY YOU'RE *beautiful*

As one of the top five celebrities who have gained the most followers on Instagram, Beyoncé's following increased by 61 per cent in 2015 alone. The graphic below shows that girls really are running the world (albeit on Instagram!).

## MOST FOLLOWED ON INSTAGRAM

As of June 2016 (in millions)  = 1 million

**Selena Gomez**
@selenagomez

**86.16**

**Taylor Swift**
@taylorswift

**83.00**

**Ariana Grande**
@arianagrande

**76.84**

**Beyoncé**
@beyonce

**75.51**

**Kim Kardashian**
@kimkardashian

**75.02**

artist rather than a singles act, and unfussed about anything so run-of-the-mill as an obvious radio-friendly hit, this was 'a surprisingly furious song-cycle about infidelity and revenge', as the *Washington Post* put it.

Tidal pitched its theme as 'every woman's journey of self-knowledge and healing'. Its title was a homage to Beyoncé's grandmother Agnéz Deréon and to Jay-Z's grandmother Hattie White. A speech by the latter at her ninetieth birthday party is played over the end of 'Freedom', Hattie declaring, 'I had my ups and downs, but I always find the inner strength to pull myself up. I was served lemons, but I made lemonade.' As the accompanying Emmy-nominated film, liberally sprinkled with home movies, had shown through its chapter headings – which moved from 'Denial', 'Anger' and 'Apathy' through an arc to 'Resurrection', 'Hope' and 'Redemption' – this was a work of poetry as well as positivity. Somali poet Warsan Shire's contributions set a worthy but witty tone. Serena Williams featured, too: nothing if not a strong woman. It was reassuring too to see Mathew Knowles in the film, any rumours of discord forgotten, with his granddaughter Blue Ivy.

The album seemed deeply personal as well as political. The references to 'infidelity and revenge' were what grabbed the focus of most media outlets. Beyoncé had been candid in lyrics before. Was this autobiographical? Was Beyoncé really raging – so openly, in public – about Jay-Z having committed extra-marital misdemeanours? Was America's golden couple on the rocks?

Scurrilous rumours had circulated ever since an incident in May 2014, where leaked CCTV footage had shown Jay-Z and Solange Knowles in a heated fight – or, more accurately, an irate Solange laying into her brother-in-law – in a New York hotel elevator, a security guard intervening to try to restore peace while Beyoncé stood by. The Knowles-Carter family issued a statement avoiding any particulars but saying that the most important thing was that they'd 'worked through it', and that Jay-Z and Solange had apologized to each other. 'At the end of the day, families have problems and we're no different. We love each other and above all we are family. We've put this behind us and hope everyone else will do the same.' There was no doubting the sisters' closeness – Beyoncé had guested with Solange when the latter played Coachella Festival that year – though the press, of course, were eager to root around for a fracture in the Carters' marriage.

Intentionally or not, the *Lemonade* lyrics, which seemed to position Beyoncé as a scorned woman seething at an unfaithful husband, poured gasoline on the fire. The track 'Sorry', with much R-rated swearing and scatology, shocked fans. The singer asks her man if he's cheating, hurls out meaty insults and threatens him with losing his wife. Someone called 'Becky with the good hair' is suspected of involvement, and soon a fashion designer was 'accused' by internet-trawling fans of being 'Becky'. Other members of the BeyHive theorized that Rita Ora or Rihanna were the alleged guilty parties. Tabloids pointed out that 'Becky' can be slang for a white girl. We'll probably never know the truth.

More sensibly, let's keep in mind an undeniable fact: creative writers use fiction for dramatic purposes. Ultimately, the schoolyard gossip couldn't overshadow the vitality and value of this landmark album. They say there's a thin line between love and hate, and *Lemonade* fizzes and hisses and scratches along that line, with a passion and flair few artists today can attain. Beyoncé has freed herself up to the point where her personas and adopted characters can straddle such contradictions consummately. Contrary to the way pop music often works, her super-stellar status has demonstrably brought her a liberation, utilizing fame as a flowering, not a claustrophobia. 'I need freedom, too,' she sings. 'I break these chains all by myself.'

Today, any hint of press-fanned scandal seems to have passed, and it's said by the BeyHive Team on Twitter that the Carters have recorded their first joint album, wherein they directly address the tittle-tattle, and even frankly discuss marriage counselling and the pressures of fame. We'll see if those rumours bear fruit. For most fans, Beyoncé is somehow both real and a fantasy figure, grounded yet larger than life.

Such magnetism and influence can be productively used, and Beyoncé has in recent years made exemplary choices. On the one hand, in business terms, she's been very smart. Spinning multiple plates with aplomb, she's progressed her fashion-leader skills, launching the 'athleisure' line Ivy Park, through Topshop and Net-a-Porter, in April 2016. The gymwear, or activewear, line was an instant popular phenomenon, boosted in no small part by Beyoncé looking fabulous modelling the items in the film and poster ads. At the London launch, dance group Syncopated Ladies – given overnight fame when Beyoncé shared their video – gave a choreographed performance to 'Formation', dressed, of course, in Ivy Park gear. 'Don't Compromise', urged the slogan on the stylishly monochrome but bustling Ivy Park website. If it was 'made for women who want to look and feel at the top of their game', it could have no more universally and unanimously adored figurehead than Beyoncé herself.

Alongside her business success, Beyoncé has finessed her fame into philanthropy and activism. She had of course supported President Obama long before her Black Lives Matter campaigning, and continued to root for the Democrats post-Obama, attending fundraisers for Hillary Clinton's 2016 election campaign. As far back as May 2015 she signalled her true colours by going to a star-studded Clinton-supporting Manhattan event hosted by *Epic Records* CEO, L.A. Reid.

Hillary was even seen praising *Lemonade* on *The Ellen DeGeneres Show*. 'I like it,' she nodded. 'It's great. I really believe in making lemonade out of lemons.' At a Town Hall meeting in Iowa, Clinton had gone further. 'You see her on TV, it's impressive. You see her in real life, you're just stunned, thinking: how does she do that? She's just amazing.'

And it's easy to see why. Although her durable philanthropy has come to the fore largely in recent years, it began in earnest around the time she and Kelly Rowland founded the Survivor Foundation after the Hurricane Katrina disaster back in 2005. This helped provide temporary shelter and longer-term solutions for victims in their hometown Houston area. Even Beyoncé's initial contribution to the foundation surpassed a quarter of a million dollars, and the charity expanded afterwards, helping those affected by Hurricane Ike in 2008. She took part in George Clooney and Wyclef Jean's benefit telethon for relief for the victims of the Haiti earthquake, and her face adorned the Fashion For Haiti T-shirt campaign, which alone raised a million dollars. She and her mother opened the Beyoncé Cosmetology Center (a beauty school that funds job training courses) in Brooklyn in 2010, and, as we've discussed earlier, her work with Michelle Obama brought two of the world's most respected and high profile women to the First Lady's campaign against child obesity. When Osama bin Laden was killed, Beyoncé covered Lee Greenwood's 'God Bless the USA' as a charity single to help the New York Police and Fire Widows' and Children's Benefit Fund, remembering those who'd suffered tragic losses at 9/11.

She also teamed up with other stars after the Sandy Hook School shootings of December 2012, in which twenty young children and six adults were killed at a Newtown, Connecticut school, to advocate a rethink of gun-control laws, and was a 2012 ambassador for World Humanitarian Day. Her video for 'I Was Here' from the album *4* was shot inside the UN to tie in. The next year she worked on Gucci's 'Chime For Change' female empowerment cause, speaking in a campaign video with Cameron Diaz, John Legend and Kylie Minogue about the inspiration they'd drawn from their mothers. Tina Knowles, said Beyoncé, was great at 'finding the best qualities in every human being'. It seemed her daughter, exhibiting lashings of compassion, was now following suit. There have been many other charitable ventures, too many to mention. Beyoncé has made the most of the fame that her talent and hard work brought her, in the best possible way.

Her insistence that 'your self-worth is determined by you – you don't have to depend on someone telling you who you are' has bolstered and empowered a generation (and beyond) of women. And if anyone has the swagger to deliver lines such as 'I don't like to gamble, but if there's one thing I'm willing to bet on, it's myself', it's Beyoncé. *That's* how you run the world. Her self-belief rubs off on those enthralled by her, crazy in love with such unwavering sanity.

Almost hourly now there is a new story about this strongest of stars, who breaks the internet with every shimmy. A talking point isn't a true talking point unless Queen Bey is involved, whether her guest cameo on a Frank Ocean album, one of 2016's hippest, is helping it race to number one, or she's breaking records again herself. She dominated the headlines again at the MTV VMAs at New York's Madison Square Garden in late August, where she eclipsed Madonna's record of most career awards at the bash, reaching twenty-four to Madge's twenty. Collecting a scorching seven on the night, including Video of the Year for 'Formation', she used one of her acceptance speeches as an opportunity to thank her daughter and husband for their support. Four-year-old Blue Ivy was in attendance, dressed in an $8,000 Mischka Aoki fairy tale frock, and raised smiles as she, unimpressed by the glamour, pulled faces on the red carpet. More sombrely, her mother also posed with the mothers of Trayvon Martin, Michael Brown and Eric Garner. Beyoncé then delivered a rousing, ferociously energetic sixteen-minute onstage medley of tracks from *Lemonade*, which culminated in her battering a camera with a baseball bat. She wasn't going to rest with the political statements, even when being crowned – again – as the universe's most potent pop star.

Of course she's much more, now, than a pop star, and Beyoncé is, as she's been smart enough to realize, actively powerful. A global icon, perhaps the most resonant of the twenty-first century, she's channelling that radiant power into causes in which she believes. Meanwhile, her army of fans – from the BeyHive and far beyond – dance with delight and march in the knowledge that their chosen champion is a worker, a woman of substance and a winner, who as a performer glows with a flawless charisma that's rarely been matched.

And 2017 began with one of her most talked-about revelations yet. On 1 February she announced – via a

**ABOVE:** Beyoncé performs on stage at the 'Chime For Change: The Sound Of Change Live' Concert at Twickenham Stadium in London, England, 2013.

striking set of Instagram photographs – that she was pregnant with twins. This bombshell dropped just days before a Grammys performance (where she was a nine-time nominee and two-time winner) and two months before she was due to headline the Coachella festival.

After celebrating her thirty-fifth birthday she was told by doctors to reschedule a New Jersey show in order to rest her voice. It may well be the first time she's taken a rest in years. She'd enjoyed a lively birthday weekend, attending (with Jay-Z) a Made in America festival in Philadelphia and then hosting a *Soul Train*-themed Seventies' party in New York. Her fancy dress costume for the night recalled her Foxxy Cleopatra look, with Jay-Z dressed in the style of Jimi Hendrix. Solange and Kelly Rowland were there, as were Alicia Keys and Swizz Beatz (now a married pair), Usher, Sean 'Diddy' Combs, Kendrick Lamar, Janelle Monáe and Serena Williams. If her life flashed before her as she partied with friends old and new, it must have felt good. By all accounts Beyoncé couldn't chat much (resting the voice) but made up for it by dancing vigorously until the early hours. NYPD officers arrived at the building's entrance at 1.30a.m. to say there'd been a complaint about the noise. Polite compliance ensued.

That may be the first time anyone has asked Beyoncé to turn down the volume. And it will probably be the last.

**THIS PAGE:** Beyoncé and her daughter, Blue Ivy Carter, arriving at the 2016 MTV Video Music Awards in New York.

# ENDNOTES

## PROLOGUE

'I'm over being a pop star...': 'Beyoncé Interview', *Marie Claire UK*, 16 September 2008

'When you're famous...': Beyoncé, *Yours and Mine*, 2014

'the most important ...': Jody Rosen, 'Her Highness', *New Yorker*, 20 February 2013

'I don't like to gamble...': 'Beyoncé: I Am... Yours', *ABC TV*, 20 November 2009

'I'm not like her...': Jody Thompson, 'Beyoncé explains her alter-ego Sasha Fierce, plus our Top 10 celebrity aliases', *Mirror*, 27 November 2008

'be inspired by things...': Michael Cragg, 'Beyoncé: 10 of the best videos', *Guardian*, 19 August 2014

'makes her most powerful...': Rob Sheffield, 'Beyoncé: Lemonade', *Rolling Stone*, 25 April 2016

'I'm learning how to drown...': 'Beyoncé: Year of 4', *MTV*, 30 June 2011

'I don't have to prove...': Ibid.

'I know that, yes ...': Amy Wallace, 'Miss Millennium: Beyoncé', *GQ*, 10 January 2013

'I'm more powerful...': Ibid.

## 1 CHILDHOOD AND YOUTH

'We all have special ...': Ray Rogers, 'Beyoncé Q&A: The Billboard Music Awards Millennium Artist Discusses Her Career And New Album', *Billboard*, 11 May 2011

'claims it was an easy...': Beyoncé Knowles, Michelle Williams, Kelly Rowland, *Soul Survivors: The Official Biography of Destiny's Child* (Boxtree Ltd, 2002)

'dad would pick...': Ibid.

'when I was little': Ibid.

'For the first time...': Daryl Easlea, *Crazy In Love: The Beyoncé Knowles Biography* (Omnibus Press, 2011)

'I loved performing...': J. Randy Taraborrelli, *Becoming Beyoncé: The Untold Story* (Pan, 2016)

'I specifically remember...': Amy Wallace, 'Miss Millennium: Beyoncé', *GQ*, 10 January 2013

'He's the reason I do...': 'Sunday Night TV', 9 October 2011

'I was the type of child...': Anna Pointer, *Beyoncé: Running the World: The Biography* (Hodder & Stoughton, 2014)

'dumb and stupid...': Beyoncé Knowles, Michelle Williams, Kelly Rowland, *Soul Survivors: The Official Biography of Destiny's Child* (Boxtree Ltd, 2002)

'People thought I was...': Ibid.

'I knew she was...': Anna Pointer, *Beyoncé: Running the World: The Biography* (Hodder & Stoughton, 2014)

'She told me to perform...': Ibid.

'I was terrified...': Ibid.

'She was a sweet...': Lynn Norment, 'Beyoncé Heats Up Hollywood!', *Ebony*, July 2002

'Her mother and I...': Anna Pointer, *Beyoncé: Running the World: The Biography* (Hodder & Stoughton, 2014)

'That's how I expressed...': J. Randy Taraborrelli, *Becoming Beyoncé: The Untold Story* (Pan, 2016)

'That's kind of how...': 'Mom Rocks', *CBS News*, 7 May 2004

'What she let loose...': www.brewer-international.com

'Karaoke was my joy': Anna Pointer, *Beyoncé: Running the World: The Biography* (Hodder & Stoughton, 2014)

'confident and fearless...': Cynthia McFadden, 'Beyoncé in a Candid Exchange on "Dreamgirls"', *ABC News*, 20 November 2006

'threatened to put some ...': Amy Wallace, 'Miss Millennium: Beyoncé', *GQ*, 10 January 2013

'I always felt the need...': Elisa Lipsky-Karasz, 'Beyoncé's Baby Love: The Extended Interview', *Harper's Bazaar*, 11 October 2011

'We made them cut off...': Dennis Hensley, 'Hurricane Beyoncé', *Glamour*, 6 February 2011

'would be rolling...': Michael Hall, 'It's a Family Affair', *Texas Monthly*, April 2004

'I would look at kids...': Rebecca Hardy, 'Kelly comes out fighting', *Daily Mail*, 19 November 2011

'It seemed like playtime': Anna Pointer, *Beyoncé: Running the World: The Biography* (Hodder & Stoughton, 2014)

'I'm so blessed...': Jancee Dunn, 'A Date with Destiny', *Rolling Stone*, 24 May 2001

'There's nobody can...': Samantha Thrift, 'Beyond Bootylicious: Race, (Post)Feminism and Sexual Subjectification with Destiny's Child', *Singing for Themselves: Essays on Women in Popular Music*, ed. Patricia Spence Rudden (Cambridge Scholars Publishing, 2007)

'I say I have three...': Lorraine Bracco, 'Destiny's Child', *Interview*, August 2001

'singing all day...': *Blender Magazine*, October 2006

'It hurt so bad...': Jancee Dunn, 'A Date with Destiny', *Rolling Stone*, 24 May 2001

## 2 DESTINY'S CHILD RISE

'He's a great father...': Jancee Dunn, 'A Date with Destiny', *Rolling Stone*, 24 May 2001

'There was a lot of stuff...': Ibid.

'too young and underdeveloped': Michael A.

Schuman, *Beyoncé: A Biography of a Legendary Singer* (Enslow Publishers Inc., 2014)

'We thought the world...': Lucy O'Brien, 'Destiny's Child: "We wear nothin' with our butt cheeks out, our boobs out" – a classic interview from the vaults', *Guardian*, 24 April 2013

'I immediately knew...': Kelly Kenyatta, *Yes, Yes, Yes: The Unauthorized Biography of Destiny's Child* (Busta Books, 2001)

'Signing to Columbia...': Beth Peters, *Pop Princesses* (Ballantine Publishing Group, 2000)

'Most people don't realize...': Anna Pointer, *Beyoncé: Running the World: The Biography* (Hodder & Stoughton, 2014)

## 3 DESTINY AT THE TOP

'This represents us ...': Jake McKim, 'Hometown Heroines', *The Daily Cougar Entertainment Online*, 23 August 1999

'We couldn't be more excited...': Beth Peters, *Pop Princesses* (Ballantine Publishing Group, 2000)

'When you're a group...': Barbara Kramer, *Beyoncé: Singer, Songwriter, & Actress* (ABDO Publishing Company, 2013)

'When it happened...': Anna Pointer, *Beyoncé: Running the World: The Biography* (Hodder & Stoughton, 2014)

'We're happy that we're...': 'Music Notes', *Hurriyet Daily News*, 2 April 2000

'I have not slept...': Eric Schumacher Rasmussen, 'Destiny's Child Manager: Fired Member Couldn't Handle Schedule', *MTV News*, 26 July 2000

'We also had a five-day...': David Basham, 'Destiny's Child talks split with Farrah', *MTV News*, 21 July 2000

'something Destiny's Child does not do...': Colleen Last, 'Charlie's girls rap split talk; Destiny's Child: There's no row', *Sunday Mail*, 12 November 2000

'couldn't handle the stress...': Jancee Dunn, 'A Date with Destiny', *Rolling Stone*, 24 May 2001

'We've been through a lot...': Jancee Dunn, 'A Date with Destiny', *Rolling Stone*, 24 May 2001

'If you've got a big booty...': Ibid.

## 4 BEYONCÉ GOES SOLO

'a weird fusion...': 'Q&A: Kelly Rowland', www.cnn.com, 4 October 2006

'Destiny's Child was always...': Lorraine Ali, 'A Date with Destiny', *Newsweek*, 21 May 2001

'It's 2002... I started...': Erika Ramirez, 'Beyoncé Owns NYC in "4" Concert Debut', *Billboard*, 15 August 2011

'really sexy songs...': Corey Moss, 'Beyoncé Smitten by Triplets, Hungry Unknowns at Dance Audition', *MTV News*, 7 May

2003
*'Liberating and therapeutic'*: James Mullinger, 'Can't Get Enough: Beyoncé', *Urban Male Magazine*, Summer 2004
'Everything happens…': Anna Klassen, 'Six Things We Learned From the Beyoncé Documentary', *The Daily Beast*, 16 February 2013
*'"Crazy in Love" was…'*: Ray Rogers, 'Beyoncé Q&A: The Billboard Music Awards Millennium Artist Discusses Her Career And New Album', *Billboard*, 11 May 2011
*'I wanted to have an album…'*: Corey Moss, 'Beyoncé: Genuinely In Love – Part 1', *MTV News*, Retrieved 9 May 2008

## 5 DESTINY FULFILLED

*'It was a plague…'*: 'Jay-Z on His Rags-to-Riches Story, Wooing Beyoncé, and How Blue Ivy Is His "Biggest Fan"', *Vanity Fair*, 1 October 2013
*'Lord, she was wonderful'*: Anna Pointer, *Beyoncé: Running the World: The Biography* (Hodder & Stoughton, 2014)
*'They were singers…'*: Miki Turner 'Pretty in Pink' *Chicago Tribune*, 10 February 2006
*'We did this record…'*: '110 Years, 110 Musical Milestones', *Billboard*, 30 October 2004
*'Who knows what will…'*: 'Destiny's Child to Split After Fall Tour', *Billboard*, 12 June 2005
*'She's the ultimate…'*: Jon Caramanica, 'Mess with this Texan, You'll Pay in a Song', *The New York Times*, 29 April 2007
*'I was terrified…'*: Natalie Weiner, 'Beyoncé Remembers Performing with Prince', *Billboard*, 21 April 2016

## 6 DREAM GIRL

*'the strength of a Tina…'*: Andrew Schwartz, 'Beyoncé Adds Spice and Intrigue to the Movie "The Pink Panther"', *Jet*, 13 February 2006
*'I'm like that onstage…'*: Wilson Morales, 'The Pink Panther: An Interview with Beyonce Knowles', www.blackfilm.com, 3 February 2006
*'a consistent plan…'*: 'Manager Refutes Beyoncé Album Delay Rumours', *Billboard*, 24 August 2006
*'a mere spot…'*: 'Beyoncé's stage fall captured on video', *Evening Standard*, 26 July 2007
*'the best pop show…'*: Eamon Sweeney, 'Queen of pop: brilliant Beyoncé is brash but fun', *Irish Independent*, 11 June 2007

## 7 SASHA FIERCE GETS MARRIED

*'At this point…'*: Ray Rogers, 'Beyoncé Q&A: The Billboard Music Awards Millennium Artist Discusses Her Career And New Album', *Billboard*, 11 May 2011

*'It's been my day…'*: Marisa Laudadio, 'Beyoncé Finally Opens Up About Secret Wedding', *People*, 8 October 2008
*'I was so proud…'*: Tom Horan, 'Beyoncé: Dream Girl', *The Telegraph*, 8 November 2008
*'the death spasms…'*: Jay-Z, *Decoded* (Virgin Books, 2010)
*'Sasha Fierce is…'*: Paul MacInnes, 'Beyoncé? We think you mean Sasha Fierce', *Guardian*, 24 October 2008
*'It's kind of like…'*: 'Beyoncé is Sasha Fierce', www.oprah.com, 13 November 2008
*'I'm a human being…'*: Anna Pointer, *Beyoncé: Running the World: The Biography* (Hodder & Stoughton, 2014)
*'I thought: wow…'*: Robert Simonson, 'Channeling Fosse: Beyonce and Beyond', *Playbill*, 20 February 2009
*'Yo, Tay, I'm really happy…'*: Daniel Kreps, 'Kanye West Storms the VMAs Stage During Taylor Swift's Speech', *Rolling Stone*, 13 September 2009
*'What I was excited about…'*: Jocelyn Vena, 'Lady Gaga Paid Tribute to Beyonce in "Video Phone" Clip', *MTV News*, 17 November 2009
*'an icon and a legend…'*: 'Beyoncé Talks Tour, Movie, Etta James and Twitter', *Access Hollywood*, 20 April 2009
*'immoral and unclean'*: 'Malaysian Islamic party urges new ban on Beyonce concert', *The Sydney Morning Herald*, 20 September 2009

## 8 BEYONCÉ AT LAST

*'I'm really proud…'*: Nick Neyland, 'Beyoncé announces her support for Barack Obama', *Prefix*, 12 September 2008
*'I never tried drugs…'*: 'How an Independent Woman became the queen of the music scene', *Hello!*, 30 August 2011
*'that out-of-body…'*: 'Beyoncé awakes her earthy side in "Cadillac Records"', www.mercurynews.com, 3 December 2008
*'I loved you…'*: Shawn Adler, 'Beyoncé, Etta James and "Cadillac Records" Stars come out for Movie's Premiere', *MTV News*, 25 November 2008
*'the emotion and the …'*: 'Interview with Beyoncé Knowles who plays Sharon Charles in *Obsessed*', www.traileraddict.com, 22 April 2009
*'We went for it…'*: Eric Ditzian, 'Ali Larter Talks Fighting Beyoncé in *Obsessed*', *MTV News*, 27 April 2009
*'having lunch one day…'*: Gil Kaufman, 'Lady Gaga Talks Hidden Meanings in Epic "Telephone" Clip', *MTV News*, 12 March 2010
*'What I like about it…'*: 'Lady Gaga's "Telephone" Video', *NME*, 9 March 2010
*'I mean, can you imagine…'*: Jason Gregory, 'Lady Gaga: "Beyoncé was shocked by

Telephone Video Plot"', *Gigwise*, 15 March 2010
*'It's definitely time…'*: 'Beyoncé Knowles to take a six-month break from music', www.music-news.com, 12 January 2010
*'the pain…'*: Jazmine Denise Rogers, 'Alexsandra Wright Apologizes To Tina Knowles For Tearing Apart Her Family: "I Regret The Pain That I Have Contributed"', *MadameNoire*, 28 August 2013
*'It should come…'*: Sean Michaels, 'Beyoncé drops father as manager', *Guardian*, 30 March 2011

## 9 WHO RUNS THE WORLD?

*'I just wish…'*: Tom Horan, 'Beyoncé: Dream Girl', *The Telegraph*, 8 November 2008
*'Everyone who attends…'*: 'Beyoncé confirmed for Glastonbury 2011', *Guardian*, 14 February 2011
*'excited to be a part…'*: Anna Pointer, *Beyoncé: Running the World: The Biography* (Hodder & Stoughton, 2014)
*'Beyoncé is one…'*: 'Michelle Obama dances to Beyoncé', *The Telegraph*, 3 May 2011
*'I'm the biggest fan…'*: Andrei Harmsworth, 'Beyoncé: I asked Coldplay and U2 to approve my Glastonbury set list', *Metro*, 26 June 2011
*'This night was…'*: 'Beyoncé headlines Glasto with energetic set', *Cosmopolitan*, 27 June 2011
*'She's completely relentless…'*: Aaron Hicklin, 'Beyoncé: behind the scenes with a superstar', *Guardian*, 20 April 2014
*'the ideal age…'*: 'Beyoncé looking forward to turning 30', *RTE*, 28 June 2011
*'During my labour…'*: Jason Gay, 'Beyoncé Knowles: The Queen B', *Vogue*, 11 February 2013
*'I am a perfectionist…'*: 'Beyoncé admits lip-synching at Barack Obama's inauguration', *The Telegraph*, 31 January 2013
*'This is what…'*: Greg Botelho, 'Beyoncé admits singing "with my prerecorded track" at inauguration', *CNN Entertainment*, 1 February 2013
*'I wouldn't have…'*: 'Interview with Beyoncé', www.hbo.com
*'Mrs Carter…'*: Jo Ellison, 'Mrs Carter Uncut', *Vogue*, 4 April 2013

## 10 DRUNK IN LOVE

*'not only allowed…'*: Rosie Swash, 'Why is Beyoncé calling herself Mrs Carter?', *Guardian*, 5 February 2013
*'[Beyoncé] leads armies…'*: Zadie Smith extracted from *Swing Time* (Hamish Hamilton, 2016), 'What Beyoncé taught me', *Guardian*, 29 October 2016
*'the only visionary…'*: Jayson Greene, 'Beyoncé's Muse', *Pitchfork*, 21 January 2014
*'had a party…'*: Victoria Uwumarogie, 'Check Out Beyoncé & Jay-Z Recording

"Drunk In Love" in the Studio in Part III of Her BEYONCÉ Doc', *MadameNoire*, 26 December 2013

'*one part officer…*': 'OTR Fashion Lineup: Diesel', www.Beyoncé.com, 17 July 2014

'*I was very aware…*': Lexi Petronis, 'Beyoncé Says She Was 195 Pounds While Pregnant With Blue Ivy! Here's Where Weight Goes During Pregnancy', *Glamour*, 9 January 2014

'*I feel like…*': Jenny Stevens, 'Beyoncé says she felt "stifled" by being a role model', *NME*, 6 January 2014

'*she made her strength…*': 'The Beyoncé Experience', *Cosmopolitan*, 13 November 2007

'*I have always loved…*': Claire Rutter, 'Beyoncé set to run the world of fashion with Topshop collection', *Mirror*, 26 November 2015

'*The whole thing…*': 'Fashion Booty', *Vogue*, 9 November 2005

**11 MAKING LEMONADE**

'*willing to raise…*': Heather Saul, 'Beyoncé fans defend singer's Super Bowl performance amid "anti-cop" accusations', *Independent*, 9 February 2016

'*We are sick and tired…*': 'Beyoncé: "We are sick and tired of the killings of young men and women"', *Mobo*, 8 July 2016

'*No violence…*': Colin Stutz, 'Beyoncé Honors Police Killed in Dallas: "No Violence Will Create Peace"', *Billboard*, 9 July 2016

'*It's inciting…*': Niraj Chokshi, 'Sheriffs: Beyoncé is "inciting bad behavior" and endangering law enforcement', *Washington Post*, 18 February 2016

'*a game-changer…*': Marian Sandberg, 'Building Beyoncé's Formation Tour', *Live Design*, 18 May 2016

'*the tallest object…*': Marian Sandberg, 'Es Devlin on Production Design for Beyoncé's Formation Tour', *Live Design*,

13 May 2016

'*this generation's…*': Lewis Corner, 'Beyoncé live review: Superstar shows Wembley Stadium who runs the world', *Digital Spy*, 3 July 2016

'*when it comes…*': Charlotte Runcie, 'Beyoncé is still very much the queen of pop – review', *The Telegraph*, 29 June 2016

'*She sounds, moves…*': Hermione Hoby, 'Beyoncé: Formation tour review – defiant, victorious and glorious', *Guardian*, 28 April 2016

'*At the end…*': Alex Frank, 'Beyoncé and Jay-Z Release Statement After Incident With Solange',: *Fader*, 15 May 2014

'*finding the best…*': Margot Peppers, '"My mother sees the best in everybody": Beyoncé on the woman who inspires her most as she gears up for major charity concert', *Daily Mail*, 8 April 2013

'*Your self-worth…*': Francesca Rice, '20 of Beyoncé's Best & Most Brilliant Quotes', *Marie Claire UK*, 7 September 2015

# PHOTOGRAPHY

| 6 | © Tim Mosenfelder/Getty Images |
| 16–17 | © Myrna Suarez/Getty Images |
| 22 | © David Livingston/Getty Images |
| 25 | © Theo Wargo/Getty Images |
| 25 | © Jim Smeal/Getty Images |
| 30 | © KMazur/Getty Images |
| 34–35 | © John Stanton/Getty Images |
| 38 | © Time & Life Pictures/Getty Images |
| 42 | © Fred Duval/Getty Images |
| 42 | © Frank Micelotta Archive/Getty Images |
| 43 | © Jim Smeal/Getty Images |
| 43 | © Fred Duval/Getty Images |
| 43 | © Vince Bucci/Getty Images |
| 45 | © Anthony Pidgeon/Getty Images |
| 52–53 | © Frank Micelotta Archive/Getty Images |
| 56–57 | © Debra L Rothenberg/Getty Images |
| 59 | © Pam Francis/Getty Images |
| 64–65 | © Paul Bergen/Getty Images |
| 70–71 | © Michael Caulfield Archive/Getty Images |
| 77 | © [Aurum to supply please] |
| 78–79 | © Dave Hogan/Getty Images |

| 81 | © Theo Wargo/Getty Images |
| 82 | © NBC/Getty Images |
| 85 | © Maury Phillips Archive/Getty Images |
| 89 | © Chris Weeks/Getty Images |
| 92–93 | © New Line/REX/Shutterstock |
| 97 | © Ron Galella/Getty Images |
| 100–101 | © Frank Micelotta/Getty Images |
| 103 | © Lester Cohen/Getty Images |
| 104 | © KMazur/Getty Images |
| 109 | © Gregg DeGuire/Getty Images |
| 110–111 | © Frank Micelotta/Getty Images |
| 116 | © Frank Micelotta/Getty Images |
| 118–119 | © Venturelli/Getty Images |
| 121 | © Etienne George/Getty Images |
| 124 | © John Shearer/Getty Images |
| 129 | © Michel Dufour/Getty Images |
| 130–131 | © Kevin Winter/Getty Images |
| 133 | © Eamonn McCormack/Getty Images |
| 137 | © Jon Kopaloff/Getty Images |
| 140–141 | © Christopher Polk/Getty Images |
| 143 | © Kevin Mazur/Getty Images |
| 148 | © Robyn Beck/Getty Images |
| 151 | © John Shearer/Getty Images |
| 160–161 | © Jeff Kravitz/Getty Images |
| 163 | © Jemal Countess/Getty Images |
| 166–167 | © L. Busacca/Getty Images |
| 168 | © Win McNamee/Getty Images |
| 174 | © Kevin Mazur/Getty Images |

| 179 | © Robyn Beck/AFP/Getty Images |
| 181 | © Kevin Mazur/Getty Images |
| 182 | © Michael Caulfield/Getty Images |
| 186–187 | © Rune Hellestad/Corbis/Getty Images |
| 188 | © Anthony Harvey/Getty Images |
| 194–195 | © Buda Mendes/Getty Images |
| 199 | © Kristian Dowling/Getty Images |
| 204–205 | © Kevin Mazur/WireImage/Getty Images |
| 206–207 | © Kevin Mazur/WireImage/Getty Images |
| 208–209 | © Larry Busacca/PW/WireImage for Parkwood Entertainment/Getty Images |
| 211 | © Mark Davis/Getty Images |
| 214 | © Kevin Mazur/WireImage for Parkwood Entertainment/Getty Images |
| 221 | © Kevin Mazur/WireImage/Getty Images |
| 224–225 | © Lawrence K. Ho/Los Angeles Times/Getty Images |
| 234–235 | © Frank Micelotta/Parkwood Entertainment/Getty Images |
| 238–239 | © Thearon W. Henderson/Getty Images |
| 251 | © Karwai Tang/WireImage/Getty Images |
| 252–253 | © Noam Galai/MTV1617/Getty Images for MTV |

# BIBLIOGRAPHY

*Crazy In Love: The Beyoncé Knowles Biography*, Daryl Easlea (Omnibus Press, 2011)

*Beyoncé: Running The World: The Biography*, Anna Pointer (Coronet, 2015)

*Becoming Beyoncé: The Untold Story*, J. Randy Taraborrelli (Sidgwick & Jackson, 2015)

*Beyoncé*, Andrew Vaughan (Sterling, 2012)

*Destiny's Child*, Ian Gittins (Carlton, 2002)